TRUST:
WHAT A HORSE TAUGHT ME ABOUT GOD

MARIE TIMM

WESTBOW°
PRESS
A DIVISION OF THOMAS NELSON
& ZONDERVAN

Scriptures taken from the Holy Bible, New International Version®, NIV®. Copyright © 1973, 1978, 1984, 2011 by Biblica, Inc.™ Used by permission of Zondervan. All rights reserved worldwide. www.zondervan.com The "NIV" and "New International Version" are trademarks registered in the United States Patent and Trademark Office by Biblica, Inc.™ All rights reserved.

Scripture quotations are from The Holy Bible, English Standard Version® (ESV®), copyright © 2001 by Crossway, a publishing ministry of Good News Publishers. Used by permission. All rights reserved.

Scripture quotations in this publications are from The Message. Copyright (c) by Eugene H. Peterson 1993, 1994, 1995, 1996, 2000, 2001, 2002. Used by permission of NavPress Publishing Group.

WestBow Press books may be ordered through booksellers or by contacting:

WestBow Press
A Division of Thomas Nelson & Zondervan
1663 Liberty Drive
Bloomington, IN 47403
www.westbowpress.com
1 (866) 928-1240

ISBN: 978-1-4908-3140-4 (sc)
ISBN: 978-1-4908-3578-5 (e)

Library of Congress Control Number: 2014905448

Printed in the United States of America.

WestBow Press rev. date: 5/30/2014

CONTENTS

INTRODUCTION

The journey described herein involves a very special horse. If you are like me, all horses are special. If you love the horse, you find yourself crying watching the winner cross the finish line in the Kentucky Derby. You joy in brushing a tangled mane to slippery smoothness and bury your face in it just to smell its pungent horsey fragrance. Your ears perk up when you hear the creak of saddle leather. Your eyes light up and your whole countenance radiates when someone brings up the topic of anything to do with horses. And you have been that way all your life.

The awesome power overlaying the extreme fragility of the horse is both frightening and decidedly needy. Truly God created these majestic animals not only for our practical purposes throughout history, but also to show us a glimpse of His desired partnership with us, his people. When we cease rebelling, kicking out and resisting His loving discipline we find ourselves in a good place. As we learn to trust Him, we find that He never fails us. Fearful reactions are steadily replaced by calm inquiries as to what He would have us do in a given situation. We discover Him a trustworthy Leader.

I had no intention of writing a book about any of this but God did. He gently pressed in with His wit and wisdom each time I felt like ignoring my horse or even giving up horses altogether. In my trials and fears I have found Him amazingly patient but oh, so direct. No one ever told me through all these years of sitting in church that He has a sense of humor. A wise teacher of mine once said, "Do not put your faith in your ability to hear God. Put your faith in God's ability to talk to you." [i]His *still, small whisper* (I Kings 19:12) may indeed be quiet but it is the profundity of that whisper that rattles you to the core just as much as the sight of a burning bush would dumfound you or the crack of a lightening bolt might throw you to the ground. (Granted, I *was* literally thrown to the ground when this whole thing started.)

When the Lord impressed me to start writing about these lessons on fear and trust, I had no idea how to start. The core scripture He gave to me is found in I John 4:18—"There is no fear in love, but perfect love casts out fear. For fear has to do with punishment, and whoever fears has not been perfected in love." (ESV) As His Voice of Love began to teach me in my spirit, I felt led to write in the intimate dialog of a letter. Truly His Word, the Bible, is His personal love letter to all of us.

On a practical point, please note that some of the names of people used in this book are not their actual names and the words you see in italics are often a paraphrase of Scripture but sometimes an actual quote for that is how I heard Him in my spirit. I encourage you to look up each of the Scriptures listed at the end of every chapter. They are of far more importance for you to read than my little story.

Perhaps you are like my horse Paladin and me. Perhaps you struggle with fear more than others seem to. Perhaps you want to trust God with your life but are afraid to step toward Him. Maybe you were so damaged by the cruelty of men you would rather turn away and kick out at everyone who even attempts to touch you and help you. Or maybe life hasn't been all that bad for you but there is that underlying feeling of dread of what "might happen." If so, or for any who simply want to read my story because you love horses, please dig in anywhere in the chapters if one of them strikes your fancy. The book is best read from beginning to end but my hope is that even one chapter, even one Scripture will encourage you to start your personal walk with God or renew a relationship you once had with Him. Above all, may it deepen further your love for Him and spur you on to seek Him who loves you and gave His life for you. It is my earnest prayer that you will hear Him more than me and realize, maybe for the very first time, that He is speaking to you, too. To God be all the Glory!

Marie Timm

DEDICATION

This book is dedicated to my Lord, Savior and Friend,
Jesus Christ.
I am beginning to realize how much He loves me.

ACKNOWLEDGMENTS

Paladin and I want to thank my wonderful husband Steve, daughter Lisa, and son Jacob for all your pushing, prodding and encouragement to keep writing. Steve sweetly foots the bill for my "horse habit" without complaining even though he is more comfortable around a motorcycle than an equine.

Thanks to my wonderful friend and spiritual mentor, Pam Anderson, for her prayers and selfless editing of this little book. You helped me get up and go on my walk with the Lord so many times when I wanted to stop and focus on my circumstances instead of on Him. Your faith is a blessing to me.

Penny Lulich volunteered many hours looking up and documenting all the scripture references quoted or implied throughout the entire manuscript. She did this, I would add, with great delight. Thank you, Penny for loving the Word of God like you do and assisting this venture.

Thank you best friend, Patti Long for listening without judging to all my ups and downs with horses and life in general. We are definitely "therapy" partners! I couldn't make it without you.

A special shout out to my friend and new sister in Christ, Deborah Engel, who created the beautiful watercolor of Paladin and me that graces the cover of this book. She is also an expert photographer and created the author picture on the back cover.

Thanks also to Jennifer Lankford for drawing the interior illustrations. Paladin and I have found a new friend to ride with!

Thanks to all the people God brought to Paladin and me over the last seven years to help us: Sandra, Laura, Lucinda, Brian, Rachel, Suzi, Bill, and many others we were privileged to learn from.

To all who were parts of our journey, thank you so much!

PREFACE

TRUST

WHAT A HORSE TAUGHT ME ABOUT GOD
If wishes were horses,
beggars would ride...[ii]
But if beggars rode horses
then young girls would cry.

For if beggars have horses
with young girls denied,
then dreams must serve wishes;
hard work not apply.

But if horses had wishes
they would run to the sides
of young girls with strong dreams
and arms opened wide.

"I hate you." I stated flatly as I stood in front of his stall that day in May of 2006. Why had God allowed me to purchase this insane horse? I had prayed about it over five months, asking all the right questions of his seller/trainer in another state. We had exchanged pictures, phone calls, emails, videos and finally dollars and a date of delivery for late March to my barn. He was trailered to us from California to Oregon by one of his trainers. As Rick unloaded him that day even my "non-horsey" husband Steve was duly impressed with the horse's regal presence.

His chestnut head sported a white face like a shield held high and his powerful muscular body tensed like a warhorse ready for the battlefield. He appeared a magical, mystical steed of dragon slayers and fairy tale exploits. In short, he was a little scary. As we showed Rick the way into our barn and our new resident's stall and paddock, Steve suggested the name, Paladin after the grisly but heroic star of the 1950's television show *Have Gun, Will Travel.*

Rick stayed in our home that night and rose before six a.m. the next morning to feed and saddle him up. Wow, I thought at the time, he really gets up early. He came back to the house and downing our human breakfast, the three of us made our way out to the corral. Rick mounted Paladin, putting the horse through his paces for all of five minutes, then dismounted and handed the reins to me. I was prepared to step aboard and try him out, but Rick did not have the time--he said--to stay for that. A long trip home and work waited there, he worried. "Take him to a trainer before you ride," he emphasized. Sure, no problem. I had raised and trained my other horse from birth. I would search for and enlist a trainer to help, but first would do some horsemanship basics on my own.

I frowned, uneasy with this quick departure, noticing a few beads of sweat on Rick's brow in spite of the cool morning air. Questions rising up in my mind were stopped short by an unexpected bite on my arm. "Oh, and we've been working on that, too," Rick offered. "Smack him on the nose and he'll stop." Unsaddling him quickly, he turned on his heel for the short stride out to his rig, threw his saddle and bridle into the back seat and was gone in a puff of diesel exhaust before I could think of anything to say. My other horse had bit me once but I trained him not to. No big deal, I surmised.

Thinking the horse just needed some space and time to settle in we left him alone in the corral for a few hours. Later on we received our first glimpse of the "real" horse. It couldn't have been more disappointing. His rolling eyes showed the whites of fear while he braced like a statue, sucking in his breath when I came near. His head flew up to the sky. Fear, fear, fear. Dangerous fear. He was afraid of my hand, afraid of my voice, afraid of the walls, afraid of the feed bucket. Name it--he feared it. He was an absolute mental wreck.

And that wasn't just dehydration from the long trailer ride--he was at least 30% underweight. So, being the 100% woman I am, I decided right then and there I could "fix" this horse. He was just a little over the top, but I would change him. He would calm down under my talented hands.

Over the next two months we made some progress on the groundwork (i.e. no riding). During that time period I also enlisted a few hours help from a local trainer. After a couple of sessions of Paladin running full speed in lathered circles for two hours in his round pen, I put a stop to it. The horse was going to run until he died, pursued by fear, dominated and controlled by it. Or was it anger? His mind was not present. Obviously this horse had been severely abused, or had gotten in some kind of wreck, or he was just of an insane DNA. Maybe all of the above. He was sold to me as having little to no experience but very "willing and kind." It was apparent, however, that he had had lots of experience and most of it was negative. The only thing he was willing to do was flee. And kind? It seemed he actually hated people.

I worked with him on ground manners and lunging in my corral for a few weeks more and he calmed down considerably. One bright morning just before Memorial Day I decided it was time to climb aboard for a short ride. I saddled up and, calling Steve away from polishing his beloved motorcycle to stand by "just in case," I pulled up a rein to hold his head and swung aboard. Nervous? Yes. But in my mindset at that moment, determination trumped nervousness. I was strong, capable and knowledgeable. Paladin was much more trusting of me now. We walked and trotted a few circles. So far, so good. Then I asked him to canter.

With lightening speed everything changed. Even before one stride was complete I heard what sounded vaguely like Steve's voice in a tunnel, "he's going to b...!"

The buck was first a mighty leap forward and upward and then all momentum transferred into Paladin's back end. In what seemed like slow motion I was slammed to the ground hard, his back feet missing my head by a hair's breadth. I had fallen first on my head and then my left shoulder.

Scrambling up and so angry that I wasn't feeling the extent of my injuries, I snarled at my poor, frightened husband, "Get that horse, I am getting on again!" Paladin had run off to his paddock with head and tail held high in defiance. He actually looked like he had enjoyed hurling me as hard as he could. If I had been in possession of a gun I know at that moment I would have shot him where he stood. Yes, I would have killed him. Have gun, will *definitely* travel 50 feet to kill this sorry animal. How dare he hurt me!

I mounted up again and made Steve walk him around on the lead line for a few minutes, as he all the while was thinking, "Isn't this a bad idea, sweetheart?" and "I don't know what I am doing, I am scared out of my mind for you!" Dismounting then, I stared daggers into Paladin. I smacked him around with the end of the reins and then I cried. A lot. The seller had said that he had never offered to buck. I had asked repeatedly during the five months as they were riding him at their place, "Has he tried to buck?" Answer: "Nope, never."

Just what does the term "never offered" mean, exactly? With bruised, maybe broken ribs, a likely mild concussion in spite of wearing a helmet and worst of all, a shattered spirit, I put in a call to the seller and told them they lied to me and would have to come get this horse and give me my money back. Response? They informed me I was about the stupidest person they had ever sold a horse to since they had told me to get a trainer and not do it myself. Well, I had gotten a trainer and he was certain the horse was a basket case needing years of retraining. I argued I should at least have been able to put the horse through the same paces Rick had done when he left him with me, which included a short ride at all gaits, including the canter.

With a loud clatter, the pieces of deception fell into place in my bruised brain. I realized Paladin must have been drugged when this guy had ridden him. (Oh, so that's why he got up early and quietly slipped out to the barn before we woke up.) Wow, he must have been drugged upon delivery, too. And now I understood the beads of sweat and the hurry to leave after giving me that "demonstration" of what Paladin could do all the while emphasizing only to continue professional training. He could have awakened from the drug dose at any moment and we would have known.

Horse-trading and horse traders! The stories I heard from other equestrians as I described my disaster to them made me realize I was not alone. Well, the sellers were not about to come get him. As they saw it, it was my fault and I was stupid. At this point, I couldn't agree more about the stupid part for trusting a person I did not know about a horse I had not met, even though I thought they were reputable from being in the horse breeding/training business for a long time. I looked up the name Paladin. It meant "fighter." (Note to self: Always find out meaning of name before christening.)

So, as I stood there on that day in early June and said, "I hate you," my heart was devoid of any emotion. I looked longingly at my other horse, Legacy, who had gone permanently lame with osteoarthritis just after we had moved to our little ranch. If he had not become unrideable, I might never have looked for another horse. Maybe being age 53 was too old for riding horses--you don't bounce when you fall. Maybe the lifelong dream of having my own barn, five acres and riding the trails for hours was dead. Killed by people lying to me. Snuffed out by an abuser of horses who had destroyed a fight or flight animal's weak trust of humans. Cheated by the sin so rampant in the world. Seemingly ignored by my God. Why did He let all this happen in the first place? I had been counting on His directive.

It certainly appeared that my predicament did not have God's concern. Why should it? It was just a frivolous little girl dream of riding her beautiful loyal steed and living on a ranch. Obviously not what a mature woman should be doing. To be sure, there were more important things. Maybe it was time to give up my attachment to horses. Maybe that is why God let this entire scenario take place. Yes, most likely He was teaching me the hard way. As if the physical and mental pain were not enough, now the dark despairing suggestion that God might be some kind of killjoy who was really done with my little girl infatuation with horses had settled into my soul.

Until, as I spoke those three words "I hate you" in front of Paladin's stall that day, I heard *His* Voice loud and clear and startling in my spirit saying,

"*You* are just like this horse."

He was afraid of everything!

CHAPTER ONE

TO LISTEN

There is no fear in love,
but perfect love casts out fear.
I John 4:18a

Dear Father God,

I am NOT like this horse! He is beyond anyone's help. He only knows fear. He doesn't even look at me. I feel like I have to tiptoe around him and even then he braces and sucks in his breath and throws up his head. He's crazy! I do not even want to deal with it. I am mad at You for allowing me to buy him. I asked You to give me direction on this, remember? I suppose now I have to believe You have brought him here to teach me something about myself. Well, be quick about it because I am either going to take him to the auction or have him put down. He is dangerous and I don't want anyone else getting hurt.

I don't like him and certainly don't trust him, nor will I ever. OK, so I admit I am a fear filled person. I see that. Fine, thank you for showing me. I am sure this won't take too long. Let me know when my lesson is over about fear. Then I can get a real horse. A safe one, if there is such a thing. I want to move on from this huge disappointment.

Or maybe You could just take away my desire to have a horse. Yes, that should do it. Silly little girl dreamer anyway. It is time to grow up. Just a last vestige of my childhood. I have loved horses so much. I guess too much. You want me to give them up, don't you? I surrender all…right? Yes, that must be what you want me to learn here—to give up my love of horses. There certainly are much more important things I should be doing. And now You are probably angry with me for using that scoffing tone with You.

I really don't care. I really don't care about anything. Excuse me while I dig a cooling hole of self-pity and curl up in it.

Sorry,

Your little girl in an old body

My Angry Daughter,

You hate what you don't control. Anger and Fear are intertwined entities. They must be unraveled to be dealt with. I know you're mad at Me. I can take it. I have some things I want you to learn about Me and about you and about us. There are many venues I can teach you through. It was Me Who made you to love the horse. Sorry, that desire stays. This is the time and this is the tool. The love for horses I have placed in you from your birth is not something we can just tear up and toss aside. Why would I want to crack your heart in two? *I give you the desires of your heart when you place your full trust in Me.* There has been a lack of that trust throughout your whole life. You are always expecting the worst. *You will have troubles in this life* whether you worry about them or not. Why not view them from My perspective? *I have overcome ALL troubles in this world.* Let Me teach you how to overcome fear and so *be* an Overcomer as we ride this out. Together.

I WILL NOT allow the spirit of Fear to have jurisdiction in your soul anymore. Listen to Me and this horse will listen to you. Listening to Me oftentimes means you listen about how I have made him. He is a flight animal and a bold war animal all in one beautiful package. So are you and so I created all people, especially women. Adam I created from the precious elements of the earth and Eve from the very lifeblood of Adam's marrow. I breathed my Spirit into them.

Then, when I came to the earth in the form of my Son, my blood and water poured out from my pierced side upon that same earthly dust at the foot of the Cross. And so, My Plan to redeem the earth and heavens and all its inhabitants from the evil one was fulfilled.

Come to the scar over My rib, beloved daughter. In your spirit, lean your head on me where you can feel My heartbeat for you. Observe. Learn My ways. *They are not your ways. But they can be.*

He is a horse, after all. I created all things. I love all my animals and brought them to Adam to name them. Not so Adam could change their created purposes, but to give them identity for relationship with him. You should have been there and heard for yourself how many times we laughed over the names he chose. Adam and Eve and I were one. I was their Father God and they were my beloved couple. They looked to me for wisdom in everything. But one day they stopped trusting Me and started trusting in themselves. That is when fear entered them and My creation. The animals fled from the fear in them. They lost their Covenant with Me. Then came the anger. Their firstborn son murdered their second born. *Anger is murder.* I do not want you to be caught up in it anymore.

There is Good News, however. My Way of Restoration provides for all the sons and daughters of men to live in Covenant oneness again with their Creator. I call all mankind to come. I call them to come to the redeeming, finished work of the Cross. These scars I still bear are for you, beloved daughter, a*nd for all who call upon Me with sincere hearts.* I AM the Bridge to oneness with Father God. *I AM in Him and He is in Me.*

Remember, *I AM the same yesterday, today and forever. My Perfect Love casts out all fear.* Listen to Me concerning this brown and white horse. Communication with horses is best without a lot of words. Even though you, a daughter, love words! I made you that way. Learn to listen to me. *See what I will say to you* concerning this human/animal bond. *Don't be afraid or dismayed.* You can teach this horse to be unafraid when *you* learn to stop being afraid--when you learn to trust *Me* more and more instead of your own reasoning.

I love horses too and I AM not mad at you. Stop being angry with Me.

I love you.
Your Father God,
Creator of All

Psalm 37:3-5; John 16:32,33; Genesis 2:7; John 19:34;
Isaiah 55:8-10; I Corinthians 2:10;
Matthew 5:21,22; 2 Timothy 2:22;
Luke 22:20; Hebrews 13:8; I John
4:18; Habakkuk 2:1; Joshua 1:9

CHAPTER TWO

SECOND CHANCES

*For there is hope for a tree
if it be cut down,
that it will sprout again
and that its shoots will not cease.*
Job 14:7

A few weeks later, after recovering from my bruised ribs, concussion and depression over people that lie and the horses they pawn off, I took Paladin to another very reputable trainer. This guy couldn't get even a foot into the stirrup before the horse took off bucking. He looked at me with one of those resigned sighs of experience and said:

"Auction. There's no hope for this horse."

Seemingly out of options at this juncture, I would walk Paladin up and down our country street on his lead rope just to do something with him as I tried to figure out what I was going to do to rid myself of him. I discovered he was not afraid of cars or trucks. Score one positive attribute, I mused. A neighbor in our horse community saw us and, admiring the horse's beauty, struck up a conversation with me.

"Pretty is as pretty does," I said to her, ruefully. After condensing the whole sad story for her, she responded by saying she would ask some of her friends about other possible trainers. In fact, she noted, there was a woman named Linda who had recently moved into the area. She had just completed several years of work with some of the best natural horsemanship masters.

5

Later that day I received a phone call from Linda. Would I like her to come over and take a look? Even after explaining to her about the two previous talented horse wranglers who declared him a lost cause, she still wanted to come. "Fine," I said, "if it doesn't cost me anything, thank you." After all, I was almost ready to give him away. He certainly could not be sold in good conscience with this violent bucking behavior. And, unlike the people who sold him to me, I, for one, had a tender conscience concerning such things. My only goal in finding a trainer was to make this horse sellable and after that search for a new horse.

She agreed and came over, accompanied by her assistant, Buddy. Evaluating him, she labeled him "redeemable" (maybe). That very word shot through my soul like a blazing arrow and struck up a curious smolder of hope. Get real, I told myself. Redeemable or not, down the road I am sending him to another owner.

Three months of training at her place was set up with the practical goal of making him marketable. She would use natural horsemanship values and techniques on the groundwork. Buddy, who had ridden out about every problem known in equine behavior, would continue his training under saddle. Buddy was fearless, she said. The greater the challenge, the more he liked it. Crazy, obviously, I judged. Hope he didn't get killed doing this. I noticed that Buddy had quite the sunflower seed habit, keeping a small, noisy cellophane bag of them in his shirt pocket. He would grab a handful, rattling the bag intensely, then chew them up and spit out the hulls right at the horse's feet. Paladin seemed amazed at this and, for the first time, there was a glimmer of curiosity rippling across his face instead of fear. Unique training tool, those sunflower seeds, I pondered.

They asked his name. I decided we would all start referring to him now as "Mister" Paladin, Mister P for short, because he needed to start "calling" me "Ma'am." I deserved some respect. After all, I had fed and housed him and treated him right for 4 months and had not killed him--yet.

Off Paladin went for "redeeming."

Dear Father God,

Can you believe it? More money for training, as if just buying this mess wasn't enough in the first place. Though I am grateful for Your leading me to this new trainer, I am only going to give it three months. I heard her say, "I think he's redeemable." She says she will find out what is under all his fear and then she will know whether he can be retrained. It seems she really cares about him and has seen ones like him come out of their bad behaviors. She says horses are generally very forgiving. If they have been trained by authoritative abuse and are retrained by authoritative kindness, they can learn to behave normally and safely.

And now, one week later she tells me she is certain he has been whipped, spurred and pushed hard all the time. But he has spirit. He would not comply with this abusive treatment. He fought back. He survived. And he learned to hate mankind.

Dear Loyal Daughter,

I called you friend before you ever looked for me. *I saw you even before the formation of the world* and said, "She is redeemable." *And so I came to the earth in my only Son for the redemption of all who have been beaten up by the Abuser of souls.*

Fear is the greatest tool of any abuser. I AM retraining you to trust my love for you. Abusers came into your life and set up a prison of fear to hold you. *It would have been better for them to have had a millstone tied around their neck and be thrown into the deepest part of the sea.*

Some abused people abuse animals. You just wanted to skip the abusing and kill him, remember? Those who were abused as children abused Paladin. Forgive them. Forgive even him. Forgive so that nothing stands in My way. *Forgive as I have forgiven you*; yes even you have abused others with that anger of yours, the offspring of fear. Forgive so that my love can flow unimpeded through you and out to your horse and others. I will retrain you. I AM your Redeemer. I love you. Your reactions must come from a center of trust in Me. A center of fear is dangerous to you and to others. It must stop.

Watch and see how this fine horse learns that a training stick is for direction and not for punishment. Dictatorial training yields mindless obedience out of fear. Communicative training yields a relationship of mutual trust.

My commands are not too hard for you. Remember, I love you. Are you ready to forgive and move on? Otherwise, you'll stay stuck. I will wait for you. No matter how long it takes. I will even wait without a "three month time limit." It's up to you. The more you say, "yes" to Me the sooner we can ride through this.

Take note: *I was abused and beaten* on behalf of "throw away people." I have a tender spot in my heart for these. I AM moved with compassion for them. It was for them, and yes, even for my abusers that I came to redeem mankind. Those who think they have it all together have no need of Me and will never change.

I love all my creatures.

Don't worry about the money for his training. It's on Me. *I provide for your every need.*

In Perfect Love,
Your Savior Redeemer

Psalm 139:16; I John 3:8; Matthew 18:6;
Psalm 78: I John 5:3; Isaiah 53:4;
Matthew 6:12,33; Matthew 9:36

"Auction," the trainer said, "there's no hope for this horse."

CHAPTER THREE

FORGIVENESS

And Jesus said, "Father, forgive them,
for they know not what they do".
Luke 23:34a

Visits to Linda's training facility afforded me more insight into Paladin's behavioral issues. He was downright scary to watch and I was glad it was they, and not me doing the work with him. He would buck constantly on the lunge line and even in his stall would go to the farthest corner to avoid human contact. He refused to look anyone in the eye. There was no aggressive behavior but plenty of avoidance. This made him a little easier to retrain, she said, but at this point there were no guarantees. Pressure and release were the tools used on him. Body language is what horses understand. They survive in the herd that way. Natural horsemanship trainers utilize that language expertly. They don't force the horse to obey but instead, they use just enough pressure to make the horse move out and work as hard as he is asked to, and just enough release by backing away to stop him and put his attention fully on them at which point he gets the reward of no pressure and can rest. The horse learns they will not be harmed but still must obey cues and commands. This transfers later to being in the saddle where just enough leg and seat pressure will move them in the desired direction and just enough release on the same aids will get them to instantly stop and relax. I began to see it but it was quite another thing to be the one in the center of the round pen serving up those subtle, almost undetectable morsels of body language because this is where I came in, Linda said. I had to begin to learn how to "talk horse."

Dear Father God,

First, I need to thank you for listening to me and helping me start to understand some stuff about myself that needs changing. Thanks for not showing me all of it at once or I would not be able to bear it.

I am trying to forgive everyone involved but still I ask why, why did You allow me to buy this horse? I know You said you are going to teach me about my own fears, but seriously, he's a wreck! I don't like him and it is clear he doesn't like me. In fact, I can see he has real disdain for humans. He is chock full of fear and, could it be, hate? He's just a horse, how can he be having emotions of forgiving or unforgiving? The current trainers say he was very likely beaten with a whip and spurred, too. That's not MY fault! I should not have bought him. He is dangerous!

Can a horse hold a grudge? Will he always simply react instead of listening to me? A horse can't forgive, can he?

Dear Student,

Can you forgive others when they abuse you? Can you say, "Father forgive them for they know not what they do?"

I did.

Allow me to live Myself in you. I give you power to change and forgive those *who trespass against* you. Much work remains, even on a daily basis. You must continually forgive, 24/7 and *70 times seven* and more. Forgiveness does not mean the hurt didn't happen. It did. But you release it to Me through the power of choice. Then I can work inside you freeing you from the binding chains of the ones who wronged you. There will always be, in this world, those who abuse. If you don't forgive, you will always carry hatred around in your heart.

The high sensitivity of a horse's mental makeup will tune into whatever dominates your soul. Let it go, daughter. Let it go. Let Me have it.

Can a horse forgive? Can a small child forgive? They are much alike, you know. I say it again, the important thing now is that you forgive this horse and even more, that you forgive the ones who wronged this horse making him bitter and untrusting to all humans. Subsequently, they lied and tricked you and now won't make it right in taking him back. I say to you, *whatever a man sows, that will he also reap.* Your job is to sow forgiveness, not revenge. You can do this because you asked Me into your heart, so *you have everything you need for life and godliness.*

I AM your Savior. I delegate you to be this horse's saving grace. I brought him to you both to teach you and to rescue him.

People hurt one another. Does it grieve Me? More than you can fathom. I give all humans made in my image the free will to do right or wrong. I have given each the will to love or hate. I have given free will to choose Me or choose the way of the world and sin. I, too, use pressure and release to turn men's hearts toward Me.

For this horse, the buck can stop here with you (pardon the pun). Will you forgive? My great Mercy extends to all living things. *I know when even the tiniest of them falls.* It grieves me also when my creatures in the animal world are mistreated.

Remember, My Power is available to you. *You can do all things through Me.* Forgive and allow Me to fill you with My Compassion for your big fragile horse and for all creatures I have made. Yes, even for the hardest of these--the ones made in My Image.

Watch the transformation that trust will wield. I brought this horse to you because I trust you with him. Remember you said you hated him? Now you say you just don't like him. I love progress.

Love,
Your Merciful Father

Luke 23:34; Acts 1:8; Matthew 6:12;
Matthew 18:22; Galatians 6:7,8; 2Peter 1:3;
Matthew 10:29; Philippians 4:13

13

CHAPTER FOUR

GRACE

For by Grace you have been saved
through faith
and this is not your own doing
it is the gift of God,
Ephesians 2:8

In the second month of Paladin's new training regimen, I was participating daily with his "ground work" in the round pen. Groundwork is what is done with both of your feet on the ground before you ever place a foot in the stirrup. Round pens are just that: round, of varying diameters but usually not less than 40 feet. The round shape encourages the horse to look toward the center, as he must bend his body to keep forward momentum. The trainer stands in the center of the circle and uses a lunge whip or similar tool in one hand and the end of a long lead line attached to the horse's halter in the other hand, thus "holding" the horse between her two arms. She "sends" the horse around the perimeter by simply raising the whip in one hand and points to the direction of travel with the other hand holding the lunge line. She makes him work hard out there if he doesn't pay attention to her. Wild running usually ensues with an untrained or fearful horse. Any moment his eye starts to look even a little bit toward her she lowers her arms and body and "invites" him to come into the center. He learns to stop running away from her and she becomes the place of rest and safety. The instant he starts to look away again and take his focus somewhere else, she sends him out to the perimeter again to work. Finally he learns to keep his eye always on her, awaiting the slightest signal from her to come back into the center to rest. He learns the whip is not for punishment but is an extension of her arm to push him forward. The trainer keeps her body focused at the midline of the horse about where the saddle will sit. The goal is to get the horse's attention off the flight instinct and onto trusting fully in the trainer. This trust will transfer to everything learned "under saddle."

Dear Father God,

I am so frustrated. Mr. P just doesn't understand what I want him to do. He runs around the circle of the round pen but he doesn't bend. His face is turned outward, as if trying desperately to escape. Even the obvious discomfort of counter bending his whole body away from the circle is not making him to yield. He is not paying attention to me. I am not chasing him. I am hardly moving at all! Fear still seems to be his ruler. When will he settle down and learn that I only want to teach him, not kill him anymore? How long does this take? I'll never get the right "moves" down like the trainer has! I have to be so quick with the pressure and release. It all appears so subtle when she does it. When I try, it is awkward and not quick enough.

This is taking too long! I want to turn away from him, too, and just leave him. I can't do this! Why can't I have a horse with more resiliency and less fear? All the training "lingo" is easy to say but hard to do.

Dear Rigid Child,

He feels your anger. Stop trying to kill him with it.

Grace is not on a time schedule. Why are you in such a hurry all the time? I AM not so but am never tardy. The issues of your heart are more important to Me than how many trail rides you get to go on. What would you ever do if I grew weary of your inattention and turned

16

away from you? I cannot. *I cause no shadow of turning.* You must also learn that fear and worry are hard taskmasters but obedient trust in Me brings true freedom. *Come to Me with all your baggage of fear and turmoil and I will give you rest; for my way is easy and My tasks for you are lightweight.* My Grace is governed by My perfect love. *The one who fears is not fully convinced that I love them.*

Grace is what happens before Faith starts its growth. I reach out to you with Grace even when you are running in circles with fears driving you away from Me. Just like your Paladin. My eye of love seeks to capture yours, to slow you down for even just a moment, thus catching a glimpse of My desire to commune with you, imparting My peace into your soul. The One who loves you perfectly is worthy of your trust. I AM worthy to be followed. I AM your place of safety. *I AM found when I AM sought with all of your heart.*

Allow Me to "send" you forward and you will find *My Grace to help in time of need.* I AM with you in the circle of life, holding you between My arms. What is outside the "round pen" seems like freedom, but it deceives. *Turn your eyes upon Me and look full in My Wonderful face and the things of the world will grow strangely dim in the Light of My Glory and Grace.*[iii]

I will never turn away from you. No matter how long it takes, I will continue to direct your attention on Me. I will continue to wait patiently for you to make "eye" contact with Me. I reach out to all who are created in My image: My lost and injured humankind. I call them. I wait for them. I did not create the world to revolve around them. I created it to revolve around ME for the benefit of all, for I AM GOD. I AM LOVE. Men will find rest for their souls and blessing beyond measure.

Did I give them ears? They choose not to hear. Did I supply them with eyes? They refuse to see. And, like your horse, all I see is the whites of *their* eyes. Some actually hate Me. They think Me a vengeful and restrictive rule maker to run from and so, fleeing My Presence, find they are hurtling over a cliff. Then--then, I hear them call Me. *I weep over them.* If only they would look to their Shepherd, their Trainer, their Protector, the Maker and Lover of their souls. I stand in the center of life's round pen. If only they would look at Me and come to Me and join up with Me.

I AM your safety. I AM your security. *My Grace is all you need.* From My hand of Grace grows a powerful relationship.

Give the big brown and white horse grace, and persist. Keep seeking his eye with yours. Learn to make your eye calm and compassionate, like Mine. As you are learning, he will respond. Soon, when you quietly move toward his head, you will stop his reckless momentum by switching him to run in the other direction and then moving again into his line of sight. As he keeps changing directions often, he will begin to understand you mean him no harm but you will and must be, his leader. This is how I get rebellious people to begin to see Me. I keep interrupting until they start to look at Me. Until they notice I hold *a rod and a staff* of correction and not a whip of punishment. Do I have such a whip? Yes. I reserve it for those who deliberately and knowingly seek to *steal, kill and destroy.* It has even turned some of these hardest ones around and headed them in the right direction!

The fearful Paladin will soon learn to come to you, to the center where you stand for sanity, reordering and direction. You are learning this as well. *When you are afraid, put your trust in Me.* Center in on Me. Your life revolves around Mine. Why are you so worried all the time about what is outside my will for you each day? Stay centered on Me. Come into your innermost being where I live and look at Me.

Be benevolent, but firm. Learn Grace. Learn to Be with Me. Learn to be like Me. Yield to Me and you will begin to change. *I give beauty for ashes, strength for fear, gladness for mourning and peace for despair.*

I AM Good.

For it is by Grace you have been saved through Faith and that not of yourself, it is My Gift to you.

Love,

Your Good Shepherd

James 1:17; Hebrews 4:16; Matthew 13:15
2 Corinthians 12:9; Psalm 23:4; John 10:10
Psalm 56:3; Isaiah 61:3; Matthew 23:27
I Corinthians 2:9; John 7:38; Matthew 11:29
I John 4:18; Jeremiah 29:13

Resisting on the lunge line

CHAPTER FIVE

FROM BOTH SIDES NOW

Even more blessed is he
who has not seen
and yet believes.
John 20:29b

A month at Linda's had passed and she and Buddy were able to make many positive steps with Paladin. Working him in circles counterclockwise he would respond to their cues, even giving them an eye most of the time. Sending him in the opposite direction, however, he braced, bucked and had fits. Most horses have a favored "side" like a human being is right or left handed. It takes some extra work on the weaker side to loosen resistance. Because of the way their eyes are set in their heads, they also have a "blind spot." This is much like the one we have when driving a car and must look over our shoulder before changing lanes.

Paladin, it was quickly determined, was extremely one sided. Approaches to the right side or "off side" as it is said in trainer language, would cause him to suck in his breath, hold it and brace his whole body in fear. It was also on this side he had what was known as a "marble" colored eye: a mix of blue and brown. One morning I received a call from Linda saying they were fairly certain he was blind or vision impaired in this particular eye, which could explain his explosive behavior when they worked him from that side.

I made an appointment with my veterinarian for an eye exam. If he was indeed blind in one eye, I would have to put him down, I told the trainers. They were quite attached to him at this point and said they would take him off my hands and continue his training to discover how far he could progress. They said some of the most highly trained horses in the world are started blind folded. This is done so the horse learns to listen only to body cues and voice commands. The lesson in trust for the horse is profound.

"Fine," I said. I didn't want to have this physical problem on top of the mental and emotional ones he had.

After a thorough eye exam the veterinarian declared Paladin not blind in his right eye; he could see fine. However, she was puzzled by the color reflected from the back of his eye when she would shine in the ophthalmoscope. In every horse she had ever examined, the color reflected back was green. In Paladin's the color was red. (That figures, I snorted to myself: Red is anger. Green is peaceful. Bingo. "Mystery Of Bad Horse Behavior" solved!) Curious about it, she put in a call to the state veterinary school. Incredibly, the veterinarian there had just happened to study this very thing. She told my vet that many Paint breed horses have the red instead of the green reflecting in the back of the eye. They see normally, but they might *perceive* objects differently than other horses.

Armed with this new and interesting information, I decided to let Paladin live another day under my ownership and Linda decided to concentrate his training from this difficult side to gain his trust there. Since blindness was not a factor, they had to believe he had been in a "wreck" of some sort involving that side. Perhaps something came at him and hit him from the right, like a steer his rider was chasing down. We could only assume certain things about his past experiences. The people who sold him to us obviously had withheld that information or did not know themselves about his early life. Whatever happened, Linda and Buddy knew his perceptions would always differ from the normal and told me I should always be ready for that out on the trail. I reminded them again of our goal to make him safe to ride and SELL. I would not be the one riding the trails unless it was on a different horse!

Dear Papa God,

The horse is jumpy and bracing on his right side, like he has more than the normal blind spot. He can't seem to trust us on that side. He is so one-sided! We even thought he was blind in one eye! He reflects red from the back of his eye. What's with that? How can we get him to trust and stop that infuriating bucking?

Dear One-Sided Child,

Did you get it when they told you that the most highly trained horses were started with a blindfold? They were only allowed to hear and smell and to receive touch and shifting weight cues from their rider. That way, when the battle was raging at night or the dense fog rolled in or a storm shut out all starlight, the horse had no fear. It did not need to see. Its rider, its leader, its master had never failed him. The cue of a leg brought a quiet turn of an ear followed quickly by the whole body. They were one. They trusted in each other. Have you ever thought that I want to trust *you*, as well? I want you to respond to My cues quickly and accurately.

Your big Mr. P must learn to respond in spite of his perceptions of what may be coming down the trail. He must learn to trust your eyes and your knowledge of the thing currently happening. He must learn to put aside his flight instinct and submit to your higher intelligence. You have to go through some difficult times together where he finds you consistently right about the circumstance. He must learn he is not going to come to harm as long as you are directing his footsteps. Even if you ask him to walk through fire and *the shadow of death*, he must do it.

Realize I train all of My followers blindfolded. They learn to move in the Spirit realm, walking by faith and not by sight and especially not in man-made religious rules.

You've never seen Me with your physical eyes, have you? You have been learning to hear and see Me in your spirit-man within. I abundantly *bless those who do not see Me, yet believe in Me*. Close your eyes. See how your other 4 senses rise up? And there is yet another, a sixth sense of the Spirit, that must be honed.

You have been taught a certain way about Me. Maybe your teachers were right, maybe not. You became set in your ways. One-sided, so to speak. You were only able to think of Me one way. You became stunted and unable to grow, doing things the same old way. My corporate church is like that. They feel safe with three hymns and a sermon and no movement of My great Spirit.

I want to do so much more! I want my people to be FREE! *The ones I set free are free indeed*! I despise religious rigidity. That's not a trust relationship! That is a self-focused and self-willed blindsided wreck waiting to happen! It breeds and feeds a spirit of fear that is not from Me. My Spirit is one of *power and love and a sound mind*. There is a sharp delineation between the religious spirit of fear, which is a tool of Satan to hold you prisoner, and the *Spirit of the Fear of the Lord*. One enslaves, the other sets you free as you obey Me.

You trust me with some things, like your horse trusts on one side. Then a trial comes at you from a direction you were not expecting and you brace, get in fear and don't listen to Me. Peace, I say, it is I! But you don't think I can safely steer you through the situation. You have a blind spot too. Stop looking with your reasoning and learn to perceive Me everywhere, in everything. You must yield aside your flight instincts and submit to My higher Intelligence. Trust Me. I can see just fine. My sight is Omniscient.

Instead of getting jumpy about the trial coming at you, learn My Touch. Learn My Voice. Learn My Cues. Without seeing. Learn to be steady. Learn to move out without balking, bolting or bucking out of fear.

Fear not!

Love,

El Roi,

Your Papa God Who Sees You

Psalm 23:4; John 20:29; John 8:36;
2 Timothy 1:7; Isaiah 11:2;
Genesis 16:13,14

CHAPTER SIX

IN THE SQUEEZE

We are hard pressed on every side
but not crushed;
perplexed, but not in despair;
persecuted, but not abandoned;
struck down, but not destroyed;
II Corinthians 4:8,9 (NIV)

There is a specific technique in horse training which reduces the horse's natural claustrophobic tendencies. In the wild, they are used to having wide-open spaces, which provide plenty of escape routes. Out there, their feet are not restricted and they can flee from enemies unimpeded. Therefore, walking into a horse trailer is completely against their basic nature; it is a dark hole with no way out. Riding in a bumping, jostling trailer is way beyond what their natural instincts should allow. With proper training they amazingly submit and even willingly agree to climb into this metal "box." Linda showed me how they began to desensitize him for trailer loading. They lunged him in the round pen, "sending" him at one point in the circle between an empty large plastic rain barrel and the fence rail. At first Paladin would panic and rush through the small opening, knocking over the barrel. Even as he got used to it he still charged through until he realized the barrel wasn't going to eat him. They started this exercise with the barrel a good distance from the rail, decreasing the space until there was just enough room for him to pass through without bumping it. They would work him hard until sweaty outside of this "chute" and then send him into it where they would signal him to stop right between the two barriers. Within a few sessions he learned the spot between the barrel and the rail was a good place to be; the work and sweat would stop and he could just stand there and rest. That is the exact moment Linda stopped "asking" him to move and he stopped anticipating being asked. In this way he actually began to look forward to the tight place where he was allowed to stop working. Linda would instantly release the forward pressure on him, breathing out a big sigh, and he learned to look at her and do the same. He became alert to her commands to stop or go but now in a relaxed, communicative way. He became tuned in to just her body language. The dreaded tight place transformed from a place of fear to a place of security and peace.

Dear Papa God,

It took longer than most horses but Paladin finally learned to relax in the middle of a confining space. Amazingly, he actually looks forward to that tight spot now. I know what you are going to say about me, of course, because You know how much I dislike confinement of any kind. In fact, I can see now when negative circumstances are pressing in on my life, I tend to panic at worse and get depressed at best. I don't like it when bad things happen, especially one after another. Why does it have to be that way? Just where *are* You when the storms of life are raging? Don't you care then? Maybe Fear's voice is so loud at those times I can't hear You. Maybe You back away and let me struggle so I get stronger. Most times I almost give up. What frightens me most is that it seems You are not with me at all! It's so hard to surrender everything to Your omnipotent, all knowing Spirit during those trials. I would rather You squeezed me with a big hug than feel the oppressing confinement of a big blue barrel of hardships on one side and no way out on the other.

Precious Daughter,

I am with you and will NEVER forsake you. Every moment of every day in all circumstances I ride out the storms with you. And no, you will not be able to hear Me all the time. That is when you really get to practice this trust I am teaching you. I am there in your center even when the pressure of fear seems so suffocating. Yes, I am with you. Press into the struggle with your spirit and find Me there. Panic is focusing on yourself and the fear. Trust is focusing on Me. Practice, practice, practice, My love. You will soon understand. Without the tight places in life you would have no reason or desire to learn from Me. Press in, I say again. Press into My Word. Press into fellowship with others. Stop and listen. Put your eyes on Me.

Learn to relax in the middle of the tightest, most confining spot because you are looking to Me in the center of your circle. The place of seeming restriction then becomes a place of rest and peace. Fear loses its grip. Wait and watch until I signal "move on." Cock a foot and relax; all is well. Breathe. I am healing your fear of tight places. I am healing your unbelief. That's what it is, you know.

You need to realize I am watching over you when you are in the "squeezes" of life. You will even learn to break out in a little smile when you feel the pressure because your awareness of Me increases. There is always temptation to run away from the problems of life and ultimately from Me. *I will never allow you to be tempted beyond what you are able to bear up under but with the temptation will provide the way of escape that you may be able to endure it.* Notice Paladin's way of escape is both before and behind him but he has learned to stand in the trial and wait for the signal to move out. Here in the squeeze is oftentimes my command to stop and take a break from the sweat and work of life.

It's ME. Not just some random chance thing going on. I "send" you into some of those tight situations in life to get your focus completely on Me. I made My people Israel go round and round the mountain in the wilderness for 40 years. They would panic at every trial that came along even though I rescued and provided supernaturally for them all along the way. In their fear, they got needlessly sweaty and all worked up. They fell into unbelief. They fell into danger. You do that, too.

Therefore choose between *fear* of the current problem or *trusting Me* in it.

Wait until I give My signal. Learn to be sensitive to My slightest command. *Happy are those who wait for Me.* Charging recklessly through the tight places leads to bumping the barriers and getting bruised. Breathe deep and wait. Trust Me in the pressures of life where everything seems to be coming at you from all sides. Finances, lack of a job, health, people letting you down, worries over family members, cars breaking down all at the same time, being alone, and on and on. My Promise: You will be all right. You will not be crushed. Stand firm, keep your focus on Me and yes, even enjoy the compressed place you may find yourself in. It is a snug place when you focus on Me. Otherwise it is uncomfortable and frightening.

After a while, the apparent suffering will produce hope and patience and My peace will reorder and reestablish you. You will come out further refined like a precious gold coin I am polishing.

So enjoy the "squeeze chute," daughter. Yes, I said, enjoy it. Nothing is expected of you there except to look at Me and wait. *In My refuge is your strength.*

A squeeze from Me is a hug that protects.

Always Loving you,

Papa God

Deuteronomy 31:8; I Corinthians 10:13; James 1:2-4;
I Peter 4:12-19; Zechariah 13:9; Psalm 46:1

CHAPTER SEVEN

BEGIN TO DANCE

You have turned my mourning into dancing;
You have loosed my sackcloth and clothed me with gladness,
that my glory may sing your praise and not be silent.
O Lord, my God, I will give thanks to you forever!
Psalm 30:11,12

One fine September morning that first year with Paladin I ventured out to Linda's place for my twice-weekly visit and observation of Paladin's training regimen. Linda had turned most of the work over to Buddy now and he was riding him successfully. The bucking was now half-hearted, seldom tried and easily managed by an experienced rider. As I drove up Linda's driveway I observed my horse all saddled up and tied to a fence post by the large outdoor arena. "Good," I thought, "Buddy is going to ride the stuffing out of him today. Now we are getting somewhere. Soon Paladin will be ready to sell." I happily sauntered over to give the horse a pat on the neck expecting, and getting, a braced-up reaction from him. Buddy appeared from the barn, fished for some sunflower seeds in his pocket and said, "Good. You are here. Today is the day you get on." The note of glee in his voice did not escape me. "No," I said, "This is not in the plan. You are to make this horse safe for someone else to ride. Not me. I can't." Buddy explained to me then how everyone on the farm had now ridden this horse. No one had come off. In fact, everyone had enjoyed it. Paladin had beautiful cadence and talent. Yes, I thought, the cadence he liked best for me was the buck. "Just get on and walk him around even a few minutes," he encouraged as he quickly untied him and slid the bridle over his face and ears. What kind of power do these people have over me, I wondered? My left foot was actually reaching up into the stirrup.

Dear Papa God,

Today I rode Paladin for the first time since he threw me off. I was so nervous and afraid I almost threw up. It was all I could do to muster up courage to get aboard even with the trainers right there with us. I do not feel this horse and I are connected in mind or body. I need to have confidence between us. They tell me to move his feet when he tenses up which will unlock his body. When I am working him from the ground, that communication so imperative for riding is beginning to form between us. Most of the time though, I see he still seems in his own little world of fear and distrust. There can't be a relationship with him when he is like that. What do I do? And why, I ask myself, am I continuing to try? Will that day of connectivity ever come? Today, I just wanted to make a beeline for my car and never come back. I never wanted to get on this horse again anyway. Why was there just enough courage (or stupidity) in my weary soul to do it? I am sorry, but I still feel like giving up. It seems he simply hates people and is now only tolerating me, ready to unseat me when he takes a mind to. His mind needs healing from what people did to him and my mind needs healing from what he did to me when he threw me off so violently that day last May.

Dear Consistent Daughter

I know you are afraid and I also know what he is thinking. I cannot have a full connection with you either when you are still afraid I won't take care of you. Were you listening to Me today or to that nasty spirit of fear?

Stop continually waiting for the other shoe to fall, my love! Your daily routine is contaminated with fear. Subconscious, it quickly ignites with even the smallest perception of what *might* happen. Trust Me. *I am your Rescue, the One who delivers, your Guide.*

Mr. P is beginning that desired connection with you on the groundwork because he can see you. When you are on his back, he can't. Your trainers have taught you to bend his neck and look at you up there. As he yields his neck muscles, he learns it is you up there; someone he knows now, at least so far, has not let harm come to him. It is a start. And of course you won't harm him, you only want his trust, just as I want yours.

I called my people Israel *"stiff-necked people"* for good reason. They were in the habit of craning their necks looking for the next life problem instead of staying in the moment, looking to Me, their Provision and Place of safety. They did this over and over in spite of My showing up in great power to save them. So they gave in to fear and got hurt many times. Believe Me when I tell you, I almost gave up on them too.

I want you to bend to Me in faith. How? By believing in *all* My promises to care for you. Look them up. Say them out loud. Did you know there are 7,487 direct promises to mankind in my Word? They are given out of *My perfect Love that which,* you remember, *drives out all fear.* Constant connection of your mind and heart to my hands and obedience to Me means safety and security for you. Indeed, My love and will for you has the added benefits of *joy, peace, patience, kindness, goodness, gentleness, faithfulness and self-control.* Supple your thought life to Me and then you will be looking at Me instead of your situational issues.

There needs to come a day when we stop running in circles in the round pen and learn to ride out. Another way to picture it is like a dance. Only I get to lead. Dancing is connection that is fluid and flowing. Sometimes you anticipate my next move with your own reasoning. Sometimes you look away and lose your focus. We get our toes stepped on. The only way you can learn to dance with Me is to follow my lead. The only way you can follow my lead is to completely give up all control to my loving arms and learn the subtle shifts of my movements.

Riding a horse is like that. Keep working with him. Don't give up. Remember, humans beat him up. That makes a horse either broken down and resigned to his fate or angry and a fighter. Some never get over it even with the best of restorative care. I know you and I know this horse. You are both fighters. That's OK with Me. When fighters yield to Me, I chisel them into the finest of warriors. I don't give up on you. One day he will look to you for his security. My desire for you to look to Me for security far exceeds your desire for him to look to you. Stop bracing and yield to My loving hands. I hold the reins. Yield. Stay "in hand." Press in to Me My dancing partner, press in with courage.

Through this horse I am teaching you, and, because of these lessons you will have much more compassion for all who disobey Me by looking for the solution to their problems everywhere but in Me.

There is hope for the brown horse. He carries the memories of the ones who hurt him and still thinks he has to fight. So do you. In your hands he will learn to feel safe. In My hands, you will not only learn to feel safe, but dance in the midst of trouble. This I promise. When uncertain, dance. That will move your feet. When in doubt, praise Me. That will move your heart. And I will be dancing with you, leading on.

Remember, I love you. You can trust Me. My toes can take it.

Love,

Your Partner, Lord of the Dance

Psalm 144:2; Exodus 32:9; I John 4:18; Galatians 5:22

CHAPTER EIGHT

COURAGE

For thus says the Lord God,
The Holy One of Israel,
"In returning and rest you shall be saved;
in quietness and in trust shall be your strength."
Isaiah 30: 15

Dear Papa God,

I keep forcing myself to ride under the tutelage of these good trainers. How I want this horse to trust me!! He is dangerous when he is afraid, "checking out" in his mind so easily, getting out of control and "taking over" with sudden, unexpected movements to "save" himself (the heck with me!). Nothing is going to hurt him, especially me! How do I convey that? If he would just listen to my voice, my hands, my knowledge of the situation! It is not what it appears to be from his perspective.

I know I tense up when he does. I am trying to press through with him but it is so easy to quit! You must be plenty tired of hearing me beating this drum of defeat. I wish I had supernatural courage. Why does it seem I can't progress at all in my mind? Why can't he?

Dear Beloved Child,

Courage is trust in action, entering the unknown. Now you can begin to understand how much I want you to trust Me when startled by a new situation or an approaching trial that you have not experienced before. Know that it is not necessarily what it appears to be.

But you don't trust Me much. You MUST trust Me more and more. I AM helping you. Every time you step into the saddle it is a choice to be courageous. Diligence, daughter, you *are* making progress!

I see what is going on in your life. I don't tense up when you do. I AM the keeper of all your ways. Do you think I am somehow caught off guard when Satan sneaks around seeking some way to disturb your peace? I AM in charge. Stay under Me. Don't bolt off. Learn to be steady both when Satan *stalks in the darkness* and when he jumps out of the shadows snarling at you. He is under My feet. *ALL authority in heaven and earth is mine.*

I know the truth about each obstacle in your journey and whether we will go through it or around it or over it. Stop trying to take control. You do that a lot. You do that out of a place of fear, just like this horse. My perspective is accurate. Don't spin out of my peace. You get hurt that way.

You have a lot to learn about My Love. You have a lot to learn about courage and so does your good horse. I ride with you. I am Jesus, your Savior and friend. There is nothing to fear. Do you know I have a horse, too? We are with you as you ride! Yes! Know I AM always riding with you. When you ride, think about the description of MY horse from My Word. He is the courageous one I shall return to earth on; the description of the warrior I desire both you and your horse to become!

"Do you give the horse its might? Do you clothe his neck with a mane? Do you make him leap like the locust? His majestic snorting is terrifying! He paws in the valley and exults in his strength; he goes out to meet the weapons. He laughs at fear and is not dismayed; he does not turn back from the sword. Upon him rattle the quiver, the flashing spear, and the javelin. With fierceness and rage he swallows the ground; he cannot stand still at the sound of the trumpet. When the trumpet sounds, he says,

"Aha!' He smells the battle from afar, the thunder of the captains, and the shouting."

You and your horse have a lot to learn. *Your cry for understanding will be rewarded.* Be courageous, my fierce child. As your horse senses your increasing trust in Me, he will increasingly trust in you.

I am coming soon and I won't be on a donkey's colt this time! Listen...*the Trumpet is being made ready.*

Love,

The Lord Jesus,

Commander of All of Heaven's Armies

I Peter 5:8; Matthew 28:18; Job 39:19-25;
Proverbs 2:3-13; I Corinthians 15:52
Revelation 8:6; I Thessalonians 4:16; Psalm 46:7

CHAPTER NINE

BROKEN, NOT WOUNDED

*Is not my Word like a fire,
and like a hammer which breaks a rock in pieces?*
Jeremiah 23:29

In November, after four months' training, we had gained visible progress with Paladin. He was showing less and less fear when being worked both on the ground and under saddle. He had become consistently reliable in his reactions no matter which trainer rode him (even me). When he had one of his "flashbacks" he would come "back in hand" as they termed it simply by pulling up on one rein, and could be stopped safely and calmed down.

Paladin would do anything for Linda's assistant, Buddy. We had seen a very talented horse emerge from the ashes of previous cruelty. Though still tense, he obeyed whatever was asked and, best of all, they had been able to ride him without any more bucking incidents. I, however, was still untrusting. Though slightly better, my own post traumatic flashback of the original bucking incident crashed into my mind every time I rode him. Yes, every time I awoke on the mornings when I knew I would have to ride. Though Buddy and Linda encouraged me to keep going with the horse, they also realized how frightened I remained. They said some people never could break out of that lingering mistrust and so had to get a different mount. I needed to make a decision. The horse required someone who would dedicate the time to work with him and ride often. He wasn't the kind who could be put up in a pasture for the winter, brought out in the spring and take up training where he left off. He would be sure to backslide.

Therefore at this juncture it was agreed by all to enter Paladin in an indoor regional trail competition to be held some four hours away. Capable and fearless Buddy would ride him. A sale of participant horses was offered without fee at the conclusion of the show, so we registered Paladin into their sale brochure to see if we could snag a buyer. Off he went on a cold, dry, windy Friday trailered with three other horses to the Trail Challenge Competition. There, Buddy would get him settled into the new sights and sounds of the big arena with his stable mates before the start of the event on Saturday. Prospective buyers would be there with the sale brochure available and they could get a look at him before he competed. Steve and I rose early the next morning and drove over to watch the show and monitor any buyer interest.

Many horses were entered. Some completed the indoor course easily and some didn't get past the first obstacle. These obstacle "tests" were very good simulations of real situations one would encounter on a trail ride in the woods and wilderness. About mid afternoon, Paladin's entry number was called out. I sucked in my breath with tension as he walked in with Buddy aboard, amazed to see how relaxed they both looked. I surely wasn't. My heart pounded in my chest as I saw them approach and cross the first obstacle, a very high bridge, and then walk downhill through a pond, pick their way carefully over three large logs and then stand quietly between a waterfall and a cliff of fake rock. Nothing fazed the horse except the last test when he had to side pass (step sideways) over some fence rails lying on the ground. He got fairly worked up then, but even so, did not get out of control. Otherwise Paladin went forward, trusting Buddy to guide him over, under and through everything. As we watched from the bleachers I could see my big, shiny gelding was tense, but he never once tried to buck or run off or rebel in any way. Points were assigned to each obstacle as to how willingly and calmly the horse and rider completed them. He and Buddy scored quite high.

At the end of the day, when all entries had competed, Paladin and four other horses came in one at a time to be showcased for sale. Buddy again took him over the bridge and down over the water crossing. Then, to the delight of the all the spectators, Buddy slipped behind the saddle, slid down Paladin's backside and, dropping to the ground, crawled underneath his belly from both directions. Even with raucous clapping and cheering from more than 200 plus people, Paladin stood rock still. Buddy again mounted and, fishing for some of those sunflower seeds in his shirt pocket, rode him off with a wave of his cap.

On our way home that afternoon, my cell phone rang. A woman wanted to buy him as soon as possible.

Dear Papa God!

Did you see that? Of course You did. Wow--to think Paladin could be so obedient, standing still with Buddy crawling underneath his belly and the whole crowd cheering! I could see in his eye and by the tension in his body that he was still somewhat afraid, but he obeyed! He didn't panic or offer to resist in any way. I wish I could trust him like that!

Now its seems You have provided a buyer for him. This is good. It is what I asked for. It is what we have labored for. Paladin can go off and be that talented horse for someone who does not have the history I do with him. He needs a rider to match his skills. Someone who will not fear that he will buck. And likely now, he won't. And even if he does, a younger, stronger rider than me will have quicker reactions, and will be able to pull him up before he gets out of control just like Buddy does. Oh, we will tell them about his past behavior and training methods, and if they still want him they can take him off my hands. Then I can look for another mount, one that is tried and true with no bad vices. A horse I can trust.

It is what I wanted. He and I will part ways. We will move on. I will make sure the new owner knows his likes and dislikes, though. I will make sure he will never be mistreated ever again. Maybe it would be a good idea though, to check out his potential new home first just to make sure he will be treated right. Yes, I must see where he is going to live. Maybe I could also write into the contract visitation rights. You know, just to be certain he is ok.

Why am I feeling so protective of him? Why am I feeling this hesitation? There are a lot of good horses out there. I must let go.

I…will…let…go of him.

Dear Transitioning Daughter,

The big Mr. Paladin has been brought to a point of brokenness. This term has been very misused with horses but it is a good thing. I guided you to the exact people I wished to use to start his retraining and yours. Do you see how the strongholds and habits of his past experiences have been *broken* up? The hard places in his mind that had seemed impenetrable have yielded to the hammer and chisel of loving and knowledgeable hands. If you had not followed my guidance, he would have fallen in with the wrong people again and likely be dead right now or starving in some forgotten corral. I see the same great changes in you as well, dear heart. Through this horse my work in you has begun to break up long standing hard places in your heart of hearts caused by fears and the resulting "protective" encapsulations of anger around those fears.

Brokenness that is brought about without love's guidance may bring obedience but it also ends with a ruined spirit. *I came to destroy the works of the enemy in my children's lives.* That enemy is the destroyer of hope. Hard places caused by him in your heart and soul are Mine to break up and move out so My Peace can permeate everything you do. I AM the Life-Giver. *In Me is Light and this Light is the Life of men.* You are in My own loving hands. I am stirring up, breaking up and creating new space for My life in you where fear and anger had their strongholds. You are beginning to understand and so is he. Though you still tense up in fear when troubling circumstances come, you don't panic and run away from Me anymore. You tend now to check in with Me first. That surely makes Me happy.

Now then, what do we do with all this broken up rubble in your soul? Do I leave you at this point to figure it out on your own? Do

I tell you to clean it up somehow in your own strength? Do we just leave it there and step around it all the time? You could survive this way, however, it would be the difference between *life and life more abundantly.*

There is a vista you would miss. There is a greater peace you would not experience. There are seeds of new life that would never sprout to the light of day and beautiful fruit that would never be formed in you. We would not ever have a full relationship of trust. And, too, the now smaller, broken up stones of fear would take on lives of their own. Let Me now clear away this messy rubble in your heart and mind. Then allow Me to water and nurture the newly planted seeds of trust into a beautiful garden for all to enjoy. Do you understand? *I AM faithful to complete the good work I have begun in you.* Indeed, My faithfulness demands it.

Would you like to stop here? Let Me know. No matter what you decide, *I will not leave you. I will not forsake you.* I love you no matter what. I love your chocolate brown horse with the white shield on his face and the white breastplate on his underbelly.

Let's give new definition to the condition called "PTSD". Let's term it now as Post Traumatic Savior-Deliverer!

Giving you your freedom to choose,

Your Mighty Deliverer,

The One Who Stands By

I John 3:8, John 1:4, 10:10; Philippians 1:6

CHAPTER TEN

COMING HOME

Come to Me,
all who labor and are heavy laden,
and I will give you rest.
Matthew 11:28

Steve and I made our way back to our little ranch that day after the show was over. We had previously decided if no one bought Paladin at the show and took him away right from the sale that Buddy would drop him off at our place. After his nearly perfect performance at the competition, his trainers declared him marketable and as safe to ride as any horse. Instead of continuing to board with them, Paladin could more economically be kept at home for the winter months while we advertised him, assuming the buyer who had called me did not follow through on the sale. The buyer, Karen, said she and her husband would have a phone discussion with Paladin's trainers, and if satisfied, would visit us, drop off a check and arrange for pick up. Linda strongly advised me to insist on a visit to Karen's property and to interview her with a few questions to ensure Paladin's well-being and further training. This I would do though they lived some two hours away and snowy driving weather was approaching swiftly.

Indeed, it was snowing and blustering on that mid-November day when Buddy pulled up near our home from the return trip after the show. He wanted me to come down to the main paved street to get Paladin since the truck and trailer together were a little too long to make the turn in front of my barn. I walked down the 800-foot gravel access road, squinting into the blowing snow, and the closer I approached Paladin and Buddy, the more I felt my heart warm with kindness for this horse. Paladin looked at me and nickered. I smiled. My retired horse, Legacy, whinnied a happy welcome from the barn. As I took the lead rope from Buddy's hand Paladin blew out a long sigh through his nose as if he was saying, "I'm home." We said goodbye to Buddy, turned and walked back through the snow now falling gently in large, lacey flakes.

Dear Papa God,

I am in conflicting emotions here. On the one hand, I am glad someone has offered to buy this horse. On the other hand I wonder why I felt such a leap in my heart just to see him coming down the driveway to me. What was that "connection" when I took hold of the lead rope? Was it the true communication I have been seeking with him? It seemed as we walked toward my barn that we were somehow on the same page of a storybook. How will the story end? Caught here in time and space, I cannot turn to the last chapter to see. They say a cardinal rule of horse ownership is never to fall in love with your horse because you won't seek a better one more suited to your ambitions. Not that I actually love this horse or anything! I feel protective of him but I still don't trust him much. I can't ride him if I am always expecting him to go into another bucking spree. They say he won't if *I* stay in the moment and use my training "tools." Why is it always about what *I* do more than about him and *his* issues? It's hard enough at my ripe age of 53 to stay in the moment! Well, he can at least spend the winter months here hibernating in the snow with us if this sale falls through. Why do I care so much for an animal that almost killed me? I have some questions for this new potential owner and I will ask them those things. Why do I sense my heart and Paladin's are tied up to the same hitching post? Did You do that?

Dear Softening Daughter,

Anyone who comes to Me I will in no wise cast out. Here I give you new insight into my own rebellious children who kicked at Me, spit in My face and yes, even sent Me to a cross. Yet I forgave them. Those alive today are no different. I AM what is best for them. I AM their home. They throw Me off and out of their lives. Some do this out of hate. Some, out of anger. Some, out of fear. Some, out of just plain ignorance. It's all the same to Me. Do you know how My heart swells with joy and love and pride when these prodigals finally grow weary of doing life without Me and I see them coming down the road to meet Me? They are finally walking toward Me willingly, pleasantly, and humbly hopeful of My acceptance and forgiveness. They are thankful to have safe haven with Me. They understand what I did for them. Are they perfected yet? Not by any means but *to all who come, to all who believe in Me, to all who receive Me, I will receive them and they will be called My own sons and daughters.* When they come back to Me, they are finally home with Me and here is where the real work begins, the work of *finishing their faith, the very faith I began in them.*

You have done this at times with Me, too. You have not believed what I have planned for your life is the very best so you turned away and got mad, essentially throwing off My will for you. The hard discipline of life's training pen came into play then, whittling away at false ideas about Me: refining, rethinking, redeeming. Just like the lessons you have been learning over the last several months.

Remember when you asked if that "connection" would ever come with him? Well, there it was as you took that lead rope and led him home. Warm and fuzzy but electrifying, wasn't it? That's the connection I desire with you. Real communication can start then. Stay connected to Me. Practice it daily. How? Read my Word, talk to Me and really listen to Me. I AM always speaking Truth into the earth, into my created ones and *to all who will receive Me. Thank Me for all things.* Yes, especially when you don't understand those things. A grateful heart is the surest path to joy in the midst of circumstance. And I thank you for being Mine. I AM so happy when I look at you.

I take great delight in you. I gently and firmly take the lead and bid you follow Me home.

By the way, did you notice how the wind stopped when your hand took *his* lead rope?

You ask "why" a lot, blessed one. It's time to ask "what," instead.

All My Love,

Your Father, Your Savior, Your Home

John 1:12, 6:37; Hebrews 12:2; I Thessalonians 5:18;
Ephesians 5:20; Psalm 147:11; Matthew 4:19, 6:24
Zephaniah 3:17

CHAPTER ELEVEN

JUST YOU AND ME

We don't know what to do,
but our eyes are on You.
II Chronicles 20:12b

Karen called me the very next day, expressing her excitement over Paladin. She saw a great horse that day at the trail championships and told me what she expected to do with him once he was hers. In the past she had been a barrel racer but since injuring her back the past year she had given that up. All she wanted to do with him was trail ride. "Perfect," I said. She would send her husband by with a check within 3 days as he frequently passed through our town on business. They had both conversed with his current trainers and were OK with all his quirks and personality issues. Both of them were very experienced riders and had ridden many horses like him.

This sounded ideal to me, almost too good to be true. Paladin would have a home with well-seasoned owners who would advance his education from "semi-relaxed trail horse 101" to "skilled, bombproof trail horse 102." Barrel racing, I said, was a non-starter as he would likely revert back to his old self when pressured too much for speed and performance. She assured me that would never happen.

Karen's husband showed up on schedule and handed me a check for $5000.00. Then he turned to leave. "What?" I said, "Don't you want to come in the stall and be around him, and see how he reacts to

47

you or even just get introduced? Don't you want to see his registration papers or watch me lunge him and show you what he knows?"

"No," he said, "My wife wants him and I might ride him too but we will wait until we get him home."

Strange, I thought.

I managed to coax him into the stall to at least say hello to Paladin. He seemed a little nervous, not wanting to even pet him and was in a rush to get going. I became uneasy. One shouldn't just drop off a large check without examining the goods. A buyer of horses at least goes over the legs and body to check for physical and other obvious problems. They were not going to order a pre-sale veterinarian checkup either which is fairly standard. A red flag ran up the pole in my mind. I remembered my own mistake in not doing all these things when I purchased this horse. I also remembered a certain trainer who was in a great hurry to get away then, too.

Calling Linda, I related what had just happened. She thought it odd as well and told me to ask some more questions and make two simple demands of this buyer so we could be sure they were not "horse traders." These reasonable conditions would be that Karen must come over and take a lesson on Paladin with Linda and Buddy so they could show her what he knows and what he has yet to learn. And secondly, they must let me come to their place to see where Paladin would be living.

This was not too much to ask considering all the time, energy and money put into his training so far. If not willing to agree to both of these requests, perhaps they *were* horse traders that would take him, make him a barrel racer or some kind of performer, and sell him for a profit using drugs to do it again. "It happens all the time," Linda said. "Of all people, I should know this," I admitted.

However, Karen cheerfully submitted to my demands and a time was set up for the riding lesson the Saturday before Thanksgiving. There would be no charge for it; she just had to make the two-hour drive over here. In preparation, Buddy would come get Paladin trailered over to their place on that Friday evening. About 9:00 in the morning the day before the lesson, Karen called me. I asked "too many questions," she stated. The sale was off. "Please be so kind as to tear up the check."

Dear Lord,

What now? The sale is off. I feel a sense of relief because it could certainly have turned out like my trainers said, and Paladin would have fallen into the wrong hands. However, now I have to feed this horse I cannot ride all winter. Well, I can actually ride him, but not ever alone. My trainers emphasized to me: "NEVER alone!" based on my fear factor more than the horse's behavior. Come Spring, I will advertise again. I'm on my own with him for the next several months for the first time in four months. It will be just him and me. Will You help me with him? He still tenses up when I come into his stall. He still runs full speed on the lunge line. He still...you know, it seems he will never trust me. I still don't have the subtle moves and skills his trainers possess. I must be crazy. I am actually glad he is not going to live with Karen but I am also disappointed because I remain afraid of him. What do I do next? Everyone, including my husband says I need to sell this horse. I can't believe I am actually feeling resistant to do that now. You're not done with me yet, are You? You have more to teach me through this horse, don't You? I am trying to listen. I don't know what to do. Please help me.

Dear Willing Daughter,

Just him and you and Me.

I am with you. *I will instruct you.* Do not fear. I am ready now to teach you boldness that comes from the wisdom of my grace. *I will give you understanding.* How I desire for all my children to ask for this. I love you and your horse. You should know this by now. It was not my perfect will for that transaction to go forward. Thanks for listening. Thanks for protecting this horse.

We have reached a curve in the road of this story of you and your horse. You can't see around the corner, but I can. What I see will delight you. But we are not there yet. One day at a time, beloved. *Let tomorrow be all tied up in knots about itself.* You just concentrate on today's directives from Me. I go before you into each day and either untie the knots or use them to *strengthen your innermost being.* If you worry, it will spoil the surprise I have for you. Please do not worry my child. I love you. Really think about that. Meditate on it. Practice not worrying by verbalizing your trust in Me because of My personal love for you. You are one of a kind. So is your strong horse.

Every day before you go out to the barn, ask Me what thing you should do with Mr. P. I will guide you. You have learned to use the "tools" of natural horsemanship Paladin's trainers have taught you. Let's work together. I have more to show you about these tools. *Ask of Me and I will answer you and I will show you things which you do not know.* My tools are spiritual and transfer to the natural. Your horse understands this full well even before you do. Your body language "says" what is inside you. Are you speaking aggression, fear, and anger or are you inviting to others because you truly care about them? Only *by My Spirit* can real change take place in you. Let's begin this honing and refining using the "tools" of *My* trade. I want you to be a witness about *My Way, My Truth and My Life* to so many of my lost, hurting, angry and fearful children. Help them. Learn to be gentle but bold for Me. I AM teaching you many things. Let's get to work. Let's ride around the next corner together.

I love surprises, don't you?

Love,

Your Lord,

The Master Carpenter

Psalm 32:8; Proverbs 2:6,10; Matthew 6:34;
Ephesians 3:16-21; Jeremiah 33:3; John 14:6

CHAPTER TWELVE

ONE WHO COMES ALONGSIDE

But the Helper, the Holy Spirit,
whom the Father will send in my name,
he shall teach you all things
and bring to your remembrance
all that I have said to you.
John 14:26

Throughout those winter months I maintained my two horses' feeding and various health issues, especially 16-year-old Legacy, who struggled daily with osteoarthritis. He would have to constantly shift his weight from his compromised front feet to his back ones. Sometimes it seemed I should put him out of his misery. The vet said if he could continue to move around enough the bones would go through a natural fusion process and eventually he would be out of pain though I would never ride him again. Often I would stand forehead to forehead with him "asking" him if it was too much for him to bear and pray for him. He would always respond by reaching down to untie my shoelaces or lick my hand and then give out a big sigh as if to say, "I'm not done yet, mom." I could not believe this horse I had raised from conception was so broken down at a relatively young age.

I also could not believe my once "sold" horse, Paladin, was still with me and continued to exhibit tension when I was around him. Persevering, I obediently did what the Lord had instructed me to do, asking daily what, if anything, He wanted me to work on with him. At the same time I wondered why the Lord of the Universe would care about all these details anyway. But every day He would speak into my heart and I had a "knowing" of what I was to accomplish. Sometimes I would simply brush out his coat or pick up a foot to clean it out. Other times, if the ground was not frozen, I would put on his halter, lunge line and full saddle gear working him from the ground walking, trotting and cantering until we were both sweaty. I purchased obstacles like big blue water barrels, bright orange traffic cones and heavy fence rails. He learned to jump the barrels as well as stop in the "squeeze" mode when asked. He steadily calmed to my voice like he had done with Linda and Buddy. Still, I could not picture riding him down the nearby trails at all. I began to ask the Lord for another woman and her calm horse who would go riding with me.

February 2007 rolled in. The weather became milder and I began to feel pressured to ride Paladin or advertise him for sale again. Either way, he needed to be worked. Calling Buddy up, I asked him to come over and do a spring "tune-up." There was no way I was going to be the first foot in the stirrup after three months with no one aboard this horse.

Buddy agreed to come over. My good friend, Patti, who had been following the whole saga so far (and praying for me!) wanted to come and watch. She was considering a horse of her own for trail riding. Buddy might have some leads and advice on the subject. Patti used to ride when a teenager. I hoped my prayer for someone to ride with was being answered.

When Buddy arrived he asked me how much riding I had been doing. Riding, I snorted? Are you kidding?

He shook his head at me in unveiled disappointment. After all the progress making this "quirky" horse saleable, letting him have so much time off was not good.

We saddled a very tensed up Paladin, who obviously thought we were ganging up on him. I was sure he much preferred his sedentary life. With just a few ground exercises in the corral to gauge his mindset, bold Buddy hoisted himself into the saddle. Oops, I thought, I never considered the liability issue. This is my corral, not Linda's. What if he bucks again?

Buddy pushed him hard right away in all his paces. Did he offer to buck? Even I could see that very thought rise up in him so fast but just as quickly Buddy used the "one-rein stop" and pulled that thought down with lightening, experienced speed. Paladin was fired up but totally obedient to him.

"OK, girl," he trumpeted to me, "now it's your turn and you are going to ride him *outside* the corral, up and down your driveway and in and around your trees! It will be just like a mini-trail ride!" he chortled, fishing in his shirt pocket for sunflower seeds.

Shrinking down visibly, I fearfully refused. There was no way I could do that. Friend Patti on the other hand grabbed my helmet and announced she would get on. LIABILITY was now flashing in neon letters in my brain.

She was on before I could protest and rode Paladin all over the place in the sagebrush, around juniper trees and stumbling over rocks still frozen to the thin layer of soil. Buddy instructed her to keep one rein in contact with the bit and to keep pushing him forward, which she did flawlessly. After crowing to me about how easy this was, she stepped off and commanded me to get on saying, "OK, now it's your turn. Get on! You will be all right. We are here to help. You can do it!" I hated her at that moment, but it was two against one. Talk about being ganged up on. Maybe it was three against one--Paladin had relaxed enough at this point to lower his head and cock a hind foot. This is crazy, I thought, hands shaking as I fastened my helmet. Buddy kept a smile on his face while he chewed on those infuriating sunflower seeds, rattling the plastic bag and spitting out the hulls as noisily as he could. Maybe I should get myself a bag, too, I pondered, desperately trying to put down the rising fear. Was Paladin licking his lips because he liked that sound or because he was planning his best bucking episode ever?

Patti held the bridle while I ruefully climbed aboard. Steve wasn't home so I hoped they would be able to scrape up my remains when I came off. Sure, I had ridden him at the trainers' place in the big outdoor arena. But this was different. This was my place, the very land where I had hit the ground nine months ago. Oh, so that's why Buddy said I would ride outside the corral away from where the incident had happened. Besides, I had to learn to ride out on the open trail anyway.

I asked Patti to please *not* let go of the rein. Taking a firm but sweaty hold on both reins, I tried very hard to relax, which, of course, never works when you try. Patti walked forward a few paces then said it was too much for her to keep tripping over the rocks and she let go. Just like that! Some friend, I yelled internally. I rode on around the trees and over the hard ground all the while trying not to pay attention to a vision of my head cracked open on said rocks or becoming airborne and landing up in said trees.

Surprisingly, it went well. I was riding out in the open for all of five minutes, which seemed like hours. Relieved to get off, I realized I hadn't been breathing and gulped in some precious air like a drowning person. My two coaches had the audacity to laugh at me. Buddy said I should not hold my breath like that or the horse would, too. Have fun, he said, turned on his heel and blazed off in his pickup.

Patti immediately seized control of my situation and said she would be back once a week to walk with me and the horse out on the trails. We would take turns riding him until she got a horse and then we would ride together. This I meekly and gratefully submitted to. The very next week we took my mountain bike with us and one of us rode the horse and one the bicycle. That way Paladin could also be desensitized to a bike coming around him. I still made Patti hold the lead rope when it was my turn to ride. She led us a few paces but then she would hand it up to me and get on the bike. Paladin seemed to be good with this training plan. I dreaded it each time but as the weeks passed I was able to relax a little.

By July, Patti found a horse from a local dude ranch string named Carmel. He was a half draft breed, very large and sturdy, quite used to and forgiving of another horse running into his backside. She trailered him over to my house where we would get on our horses and ride out. When I felt Paladin getting tense, especially when we were heading toward home and he would pick up speed, I would simply turn him around with the one rein "tool" and put him on Carmel's tail. There he would settle down and walk calmly again.

Prayer answered.

I never rode alone that year. I was so blessed to have Patti and Carmel for company. We rode once or twice a week well into autumn. As winter set in, Patti declared she was a fair weather rider. I decided I would be also and had Paladin's shoes removed. He and I returned to his ground work in the corral as weather permitted until the following spring.

Dear Papa God,

As You are well aware, I am still afraid of Mr. P. He has a lot of power to hurt me. If I were You, I would be really tired of hearing the same whine over and over from me. So hear me as I thank you for a friend to help me get out there and ride. I would never have the courage to ride this horse alone. Paladin really likes Carmel. He seems to have some kind of respect for him.

You are still pushing me forward with this horse. I am sorry You have so much work to do in me concerning fear and trust. At this point I could get discouraged (and do), as it would seem I am learning so slow. I feel my resistance, just like I feel his. OK, teach on. I am not sure if Paladin and I will part ways anytime soon, but I leave that up to You. I am learning to live in the moment more but continue to get my stomach in a bind before we ride. Thank you for every successful ride and every safe return to the barn. And thank you for my friend, Patti.

Dear Obedient Daughter,

I never grow weary hearing your voice, even when you whine. I never lose patience with your struggle. Trust My power over Mr. P's. With the horse, the more you let go, relaxing down into your seat and becoming one with him, the greater your safety. So it is with your relationship with Me. Be in the moment with Me. *My power is very great toward those who believe Me.*

Do you remember how you loved to watch "The Lone Ranger" every Saturday morning as a child? Though he was a bold man he always had Tonto to help him. Without Tonto and his horse Scout, nothing could have been a success. Indeed, Tonto's advice always contributed to the outcome of victory. No one really gave him much credit though. So, you see, the masked man was never really a loner.

You love to operate in your own strength. So does your horse. When others let you down enough times in this life, it is an understandable reaction to "protect" yourself. But you must work with Me and with those I bring into your life. I have no "lone rangers" in My kingdom. Where one is weak, another is strong. Where one lacks wisdom, another has experience to teach and lead. *I call my people to bear one another's burdens and so fulfill the will of Christ.*

No loners in the pack. No mavericks in the herd. No strays in the flock. Those who act alone are vulnerable to the enemy. *I AM the one who comes alongside. I AM your Helper.* I show Myself abundantly in and through your spiritual sisters and brothers. I need you to understand this so you will love others by coming alongside them when they are weak and riding out the situations of life, sometimes taking that lead rope to get them going. Those who stumble and those who are runaways and those who are weak in any way will learn to rely on Me and My strength. I need your participation in the trail ride of life. I don't need you to be a loner. I need you to care and to care deeply for my own.

See how I brought my daughter Patti to help you. I literally put her alongside you. You appreciate her being there, and Paladin loves having another horse that is confident to instill the same in him.

As for those remnant thoughts of fear you still experience, do you realize how far I have brought you along this road of trust? Take a look back over the last year! Your Mr. P did not buck after all that time off! And, with encouragement from your friend, you were able to push aside those doom filled estimations of your situation and get on him. *Take every thought captive beloved, and make those thoughts obey Me.* How many times have I said to my people through the millennia, *trust and do not be afraid.*

Practice stabilizing your thought life. *Whatever is true, whatever is worthy of reverence, and is honorable and seemly, whatever is just, whatever is pure, whatever is lovely and lovable, whatever is kind and winsome and gracious, if there is any virtue and excellence, if there is anything worthy of praise, think on and weigh and take account of these things.* Fix your mind on them.

I am so pleased with my daughters who are riding together and helping each other grow in confident trust in Me. *For where two or more of you are gathered in My Name, there am I with them.* That includes gathering together on horseback.

I listen and enjoy your conversations as you ride and, by the way, go get yourself a bag of sunflower seeds.

Love,

Your Parakletos,

The One Who Comes Alongside

> *Ephesians 3:14-21; 6:10; Galatians 6:2; John 14:16;*
> *2 Corinthians 10:5b; Isaiah 41:10; 2 Timothy 1:7;*
> *Philippians 4:8; Matthew 18:20; Malachi 3:16-17*

Patti and Carmel were such a blessing to Paladin and me.

CHAPTER THIRTEEN

FLEXIBLE

Blessed is the one who listens to Me
watching daily at my gates,
waiting beside my doors.
Proverbs 8:34

Paladin's training continued on throughout the winter of 2007/2008 with the usual groundwork, reviewing all we had accomplished the year before. Even so, he remained explosive at times.

In January of 2008, I was in need of a new farrier for my horses. The same people who had connected us with Buddy linked me with Bill. He came for our first shoeing appointment and was very patient and kind to my nervous Paladin who never trusted a new person coming into his life. As it turned out he also started colts and took on a few "problem" horses. Since Buddy was no longer operating out of Linda's barn, I asked Bill to come over the following week to evaluate Paladin. He worked him 15 minutes or so on the lunge line and Paladin responded to him quickly and respectfully. Bill said he had access to a private indoor riding arena just two miles away so in February I gingerly trailered Paladin over the snowy/icy roads for a lesson.

Bill rode him half of the one-hour lesson and videotaped me riding during the second half, which was very helpful. First, because I could see I actually looked good and sat well on the horse and second, I saw where I needed improvement. This was especially apparent with my hands. I had ridden for 12 years only on my Legacy, who never did anything to hurt me, but who loved to go fast and could be very headstrong. Consequently, I had developed the habit of "hard" hands, which is riding with overzealous rein control. Bill made me put a lot of slack in my reins and taught me to be quicker with the one-rein stop, all of which caused me to sit deeper in the saddle, a much more secure position. It also gave me the "brake" I had needed for Paladin when he chose to get strong with me.

We set up lessons weekly for the next three months. After that, with a bit more confidence and the OK from Bill to even ride alone at times, I went out on the trails once more with Patti and other various riding companions while still reviewing groundwork principles a couple of days a week. I was able to ride well into autumn again without any negative incidents.

Dear Papa God,

Thank you so much for bringing Bill into our path. He has a slightly different perspective than the last trainers, but it seems we are on a continuum with what we have learned so far.

It sure has been great having Patti to ride with again and others You have led me too, as well. They all have their "advice" for me to get over my fears (or trade this horse for another).

Case in point: Paladin always wants things done the same time in the same way. When I put on his fly mask, he figures it's certainly time for pasture turnout. If I want to ride him at 1:00 pm, and he has been used to going only at 10:00 am, he seems irritated. If I change anything in his routine and pattern, he gets ornery and full of himself. Pushy, even. It makes me feel unsafe. Remind me again why I am spending all this time training an animal that is way too smart for his tiny brain? Or should I say, too self-focused to pay attention to me? I need him listening to me at all times when I ride. Otherwise he will try to take control and I could get hurt again. I need him to go when I say go and have it not matter what time of day or even night. Rigidity is not only boring, but also when he won't yield to my plan for the day,

I feel so disrespected and know he will transfer that unwillingness to being under saddle. That means me in the saddle being ignored and that will most certainly lead to an accident. It's discouraging.

Dear Child of Habits,

You know by now what I will say: You are just like that, too. Is he looking for you when you come out to the barn or is he looking for what you can do for him? Are you looking for Me each morning or are you looking only for what I can do for you?

You like your routine. You like things to stay the same. This kind of security is not in Me but in the routine, which you have planned, in all its restrictive detail. Self-center is not God-centered and is unsafe and unsound. Be ready in "your" day to be interrupted by Me. *Each day is a day I have made* and already figured everything out for you. They are *My* days made for My glory and your benefit. I form each one of them uniquely for you and all mankind to live in abundantly. I offer you My plan for your best in each day.

Welcome "side trips" if they are from Me. Reject them if not. Learn to discern the difference. Horses are routine loving animals. They like things to be predictable and so do you. There is a good and happy element to habits when they *promote life and godliness*. When they become the goal in themselves however, they become gods unto you that control you by fear of doing anything out of the ordinary.

You don't like it when I ask you to change direction; your plans for the day are made and if anything interrupt, you get mad. Notice how fear rides double with anger in the saddle. Yes, my beloved, we are looking at fear again. Recognize this spirit still exercising its false control over you. Also recognize that you have come a long way in courage since we began this journey.

Re-cut your patterns with this horse. Do things a little out of routine each day. Check often to see if he is listening to you or to what he thinks you are going to do or not do. You will thereby intrigue his mind to look to you for direction at all times.

The big picture for you and my people is this: I want them to look to Me and not to patterns of false safety in the traditions of man's religion. I cannot be put in a religion box. *I never go against My own Word and I AM constantly doing a new thing!* My creative power is limitless and always governed by My love.

Rigidity and consistency is not the same thing. Consistency is good. Be consistent to read My Word daily and meet with Me first thing in the morning, listening to My instructions for the day. But be obedient to change your course at My Will. There are beautiful vistas I want to share with you that we could not see together if we stayed on the same old trails all the time.

Do that on a ride. You want to make sure he is paying attention to you and not simply plodding along so you move him around a stump or back the way you came to see where his mind is. Just to see if he is listening. So likewise I might steer you in an unexpected direction. Maybe for a purpose to help someone crying out to Me for help or maybe for no known reason at all except to see where your will is. Do you trust Me? Are you ready to comply? Will you go only because I asked? Will you go the second mile for Me? Will you go on a trail away from home's direction, a trail away from the security of the barn? Am I your security or do your habits and routines become more important than Me? Is it how you think things are or how I say they are?

Just checking. Are your listening to Me? Are we one together? Are you *watching daily for My instructions?* Are you listening to My plans for the day? They will watch over you and keep you safe.

By the way, the size of his brain is the perfect ratio to the strength of his body. *Who are you to critique what I have made,* my love?

Remember, I made you both.

Your Papa God,

Creator of each new moment

Psalm 188:24; Isaiah 43:19;
Habakkuk 2:1; Proverbs 8:33-36; Job 40:1

CHAPTER FOURTEEN

WORKING TOGETHER

God sovereignly made me—the first, the basic—
before he did anything else.
I was brought into being a long time ago,
well before Earth got its start.
I arrived on the scene before Ocean,
yes, even before Springs and Rivers and Lakes.
Before Mountains were sculpted and Hills took shape,
I was already there, newborn;
Long before God stretched out Earth's Horizons,
and tended to the minute details of Soil and Weather,
And set Sky firmly in place,
I was there.
When he mapped and gave borders to wild Ocean,
built the vast vault of Heaven,
and installed the fountains that fed Ocean,
When he drew a boundary for Sea,
posted a sign that said no trespassing,
And then staked out Earth's Foundations,
I was right there with him, making sure everything fit.
Day after day I was there, with my joyful applause,
always enjoying his company,
Delighted with the world of things and creatures,
happily celebrating the human family.
Proverbs 8:22-31, The Message

Dear Papa God,

Today I should have ridden Paladin but I think too much about it, and then get uptight and scared. Sorry for complaining again. I think and then I whine. Even I am tired of me. If I didn't know You were teaching me through this horse I would have sold or given him away by now. If I had a dollar for every time some horse person said to me, "Life is short--ride a good horse" I would have enough to buy that good horse. Anyway, I chickened out on our ride again. That bond between this horse and me, well, I don't see it coming under saddle. Not the way I imagine it should be. But the bond of fear certainly tightens back up when I can't muster up courage to ride alone. No wonder my mother read the same book over and over to me before bed called *Fraidy Cat*.[iv] Even as a small child I was dealing with fear way too much. I was on my own most of the time, thinking my own child thoughts and unfortunately, lacking the affirmation of even a small parental hug. I guess you are delving into my past a little to make me see possible roots of my fears. Well, back to today. Instead of riding him and being beyond weary of the conflict in my head over it, I decided to slap some stain on the corral fence and at least accomplish something horse related which didn't require much thinking. I had to do it before autumn anyway. Nothing like a warm day in July to do some painting, and I like to paint.

While slathering red stain on the fence rails and just as much on myself, I noticed out of the corner of my eye Paladin observing me from the far end of the corral. Ignoring him and letting my mind wander back and forth with the strokes of the paintbrush, I turned slightly to dip the brush in the can and was startled when there he was right behind me, soft muzzle blowing inquisitively. Staying on one knee I blew back just as softly at him and continued to paint and talk to him about nothing in particular.

You know, he just hung out with me. He didn't snort and run off but followed me along each section of fence like my supervisor. Maybe he was mesmerized by the long brush strokes. Maybe he liked me beneath him for once instead of in the saddle. I had to trust him not to bite me or run over me. I wanted to think he actually liked being with me for once. It was as if we were friends who could just hang out together without saying anything--me working and he enjoying the progress of the brush. Could this be the start of the bond I have been looking for? I was touched deeply as I realized this is what You want from *me*: trusting companionship.

My Friend,

Could you just come and hang out with Me sometimes? Just *Be* with Me? With no expectations? No words needed? To watch what I AM doing? I AM working all the time. I love when you come to watch over my shoulder. I, Your LORD, painted the world with marvelous colors and also came as a humble servant, staining My very life-giving blood on a splintery wooden cross. All for you, all for every soul, all for Love. Why? Because humankind turned away from walking with Me to themselves and other gods *whose paths may seem right but which end in their eternal death.*

I called Abraham my friend. And Moses. And David. My disciple John was the one who wanted only to lean his head on my shoulder and just be with Me. Mary's desire was simply to sit at my feet. So much is said without words. These and many others obeyed My commandments because they loved Me. They learned to feel safe with Me and I let them help Me in My Kingdom work.

Trust is the foundation for glad obedience, which builds relationship, which builds friendship, which builds more trust. True friendship is the best. The side-by-side kind. Arm in arm. Heart to heart. Tested, tried and true. Without that first step of trust, it never happens.

Isn't it wonderful to have your good horse come to your side while you work, choosing to be where you are? *A curious mind that seeks Me is rewarded.* Yes, and that is the lesson here for you. Now you understand. Follow along with Me and watch and then participate in My work. Enjoy what I am doing. Enjoy my quiet Presence. Enjoy our friendship. Enjoy Me. Fear cannot abide where love binds two hearts together. Trust in My love for you.

Your horse is beginning to feel safe with you, safer than being on his own. He is standing on the threshold of entering into secure friendship with you. Bid him come. Learn to be an "inviting" person. As you do this with people, they will be attracted and curious to know what we are doing together.

Rest assured. I AM your friend. *I laid down my Life for My Friends.* Will you still run in fear from Me? Or will you come and be *and remain in My love?* I, even your GOD, *no longer call you servant, but friend!*

Tomorrow, let's get you to push aside the fear again. Let's take a break from staining the fence and go for a ride! Together! You will be OK. Stay close to My shoulder. Stay close enough to hear Me speaking about this, or that.

I enjoy you and your horse. And good job on the fence.

Love,

The Friend Who Sticks Closer Than A Brother
Proverb 8:17; 14:12; 16:25; 18:24b;
John 15:9,13,15

CHAPTER FIFTEEN

WHENEVER, WHATEVER

Do all things
without grumbling
or questioning
Philippians 2:14

Dear Jesus,

It does really help to imagine You with us as we ride. After all, You said You would *never leave me or forsake me.* People think I am crazy to say You ride with us. Well, I believe You do.

Even so, I still have issues with Paladin's attitude. I should be able to go out to the barn, saddle him up and ride away without any fuss or even a second thought. But I start to worry. I think he is not happy to go and might act up. When I come to retrieve him for a ride he runs out to the farthest point of the corral. I wish I had a whatever, whenever, no questions asked kind of horse--any weather, any time, anywhere. You know, the kind I always saw in the old TV western shows. I shouldn't have to go over the basics every time with him before each ride! He's just a horse but it seems to me he is grumbling when I ask him to do any work at all, especially when it is a different time of day or I am teaching him something new. I do not ask a lot of him. A couple of times a week carrying me down the trails for an hour or two should be more than OK when he gets such awesome care from me. All his needs are met. Where's the gratitude? Where's the love? Why the attitude?

Dear Daughter,

You know, you should be able to be interrupted and "saddled up," so to speak, with my directive anytime, anywhere, whenever, wherever, whatever is asked of you. But we are not to that point yet, are we? So let's go over the basics again, dear heart. I want from you also the easy response, easy obedience; yes, even the happy obedience. That's what I'm doing within your heart, *working and willing My own good pleasure in you.* My desire is for you to want to do whatever is requested of you. What's your desire? Grumbling and complaining is frustrating, isn't it? How much better if Paladin ran up to you, stuck his nose in the halter and said, "What's on the agenda today, mom?" That can and will happen if you don't give up.

On to maturity. Trust Me. I work in your spirit causing you to be able to trust. *I make you competent, not by rules, but by my Spirit.* Be my wherever, whenever, whatever carrier of My Presence and purposes. Circumstances and feelings must not rule you. Rise above them in my Spirit. *What I ask of you is not too hard.*

Don't stay in the place of worry and fear wondering what is going to happen or not happen. Learn by practice to stay in My Love and believe beyond your feelings. Fear loses its power when it is not given attention. Give attention only to My words and promises and promptings of My Spirit.

Grumbling and complaining is unbelief in Me.

Do not be afraid. Only believe. Carry My Spirit willingly. After all I have done and continue to do for you is it too much to try? Think on and remember all I AM and have provided for you. Yes, this is how you get there, by being thankful. Think on My *loving kindness and mercy and long suffering.* Let gratitude fill you up and leave no room for a murmuring and ungrateful attitude.

Love,

Your Whenever, Whatever, Wherever, Anytime, Anywhere,

Merciful Savior God

Deuteronomy 31:8; Philippians 2:13;
2 Corinthians 3:6; Matthew 11:30; Romans 2:4

CHAPTER SIXTEEN

THE STUFF ON THE SADDLE

No test or temptation that comes your way
is beyond the course of what others have had to face.
All you need to remember is that God will never let you down;
he'll never let you be pushed past your limit;
he'll always be there to help you come through it.
I Corinthians 10:13 (The Message)

Dear Jesus,

Today I saddled up and worked Paladin in the corral. I attached a big plastic bag to the horn of the saddle and made him walk, trot and canter on the lunge line. The faster he went, the more noise the bag made and the tenser he became. He could hear it more than he could see it and what he could see of it was the billowing end as the bag filled with air. It sounded scary for sure. That was the whole point, to desensitize him to new and potentially scary things that could get caught on the saddle or blow around us during a trail ride.

BUT! For the very first time in his training, he did not race out mindlessly. He didn't even start bucking to rid himself of the bag "demon!" For the very first time on the lunge line, he listened to me over and above the noise of the bag! For the first time, he cocked an ear to hear my voice over his fear. He looked to me and saw I was not perplexed by this unexpected monster. This is awesome indeed and so very satisfying. I think he just made a big leap in his trust of me.

Dear Progressing Daughter,

Yes! Awesome! Now you understand how I rejoice when your first reaction is to listen to *My* voice in a sudden turn of events instead of getting in fear and wondering what bad thing is attacking! I heard you say to Paladin, "Good boy, I see the bad bag. It's OK! I see it and you are all right." I have said that to you so many times but you couldn't hear me over your panic. When a burden attaches itself to you or something happens in your life that seems frightening, please understand I can see it for what it *really* is. Remember! Say to yourself each time: Fear is False Evidence Appearing Real. What your horse perceives as a monster on the saddle is just a plastic bag. You know it but he doesn't. You say it's nothing to fear and he has to reach a point in his trust in you to agree even though everything in him says to flee the thing and not believe what you say. I want you to believe what I say to you. Relax and listen to Me first when the unexpected happens to you. Do for Me what you want him to do: Turn an ear, give Me an eye. I see it and maybe I even put it there on purpose.

Under all "circumstances," TRUST. How I am thrilled and satisfied when you listen to Me in spite of all the surrounding "noise." My heart thrills when I see you connect to Me immediately in trust even though you don't understand what is going on. Even though you are afraid. *When you are afraid, put your trust in Me.*

I AM your Peace, your Place of safety, and your strong Deliverer. *You need not fear the terror of the night nor the arrow that flies by day nor the pestilence that stalks in darkness nor the destruction that wastes at noonday because I AM the Most High, your shelter and your Secret Place.* You are under My personal care.

Love,

EL ROI,

Your God, Who Sees You

Psalm 56:3,11; John 14:1; Psalm 91:5-10a; Exodus 16

Paladin finally learned to relax and give me an eye

CHAPTER SEVENTEEN

THE STUFF IN THE SHADOWS

Then I saw heaven opened,
and behold, a white horse!
The one sitting on it is called
Faithful and True,
Rev. 19:11a

It had now been over two years since Paladin arrived on our ranch. It was Autumn of 2008, and with another cold winter coming I simply let Paladin hibernate again with his equine buddies. I worked him in my corral on the lunge line as weather permitted. We made further progress and I became slightly more confident though fear still came to badger and test me.

By April of the following year I was seeking new women to ride with. My friend Patti made a decision to stop riding when she had, of all things, been bucked off Carmel while riding in her pasture. She had sustained broken ribs and a severely bruised shoulder. In addition, an old kidney injury had been aggravated by the slam to the ground. Her doctor strongly advised her to end all equestrian activities. This turn of events was very sad for us both.

Though I had been riding alone a few times the previous summer, I consulted with Bill again about all this. We took a few refresher lessons with him. Bill was confident of the progress Paladin and I had made out on the trails and thought it acceptable to go alone now anytime, but always let someone know when I left and came back.

73

I tried to find a riding companion as much as possible but found it difficult to connect with other people's busy lives. I had to muster everything in me to put aside fear and do the solo rides. Anyone who has been bucked off even one time has a tremendous uphill climb gaining confidence again, especially on the horse that did the bucking. I was weary of battling my fear, but at the same time was compelled in my spirit by God to do so. After all, He promised to always be with me. He was continually "training" me through this horse, so quitting was not an option. I devised a safety plan. I would leave messages on Steve's cell phone when he was at work as to my departure times and estimated arrivals back at the barn. Then I would lead Paladin out to the trails, and armed with a pocket full of horse treats, I would let him munch on one as I mounted up to begin my rides. We would stop along the way and I would reach down to give him another treat. This rewarded him for stopping whenever I asked. I chattered away to him as we went and even broke into singing, too, along the way. There was no one but Jesus and the horse to listen to it. Chewing calmed Paladin and singing calmed me so we both stayed focused.

During these solo rides we often ran into some kind of odd situation. I began to think the Lord was orchestrating these events, testing both of us to show us that He was the one in control. One time it was an old man jogging toward us dressed in a white T-shirt and white shorts and yes, white shoes. To top it off, he was carrying a white plastic grocery bag, which rattled noisily as he came. I was surely glad we had worked with the bag on the saddle, but this time it was heading right for us. Paladin froze in place, ready to bolt. The man seemed oblivious to us. I blurted out to him to please say something, anything! When he did, Paladin blew out his air in relief like a popped balloon (whew! No monster! Monsters don't speak human talk.) We never saw that man again on the trail. Another time it was a boy on a bicycle with his coat billowing like a sail. Still another time it was a dog...

Dear Lord Jesus,

Today, I asked You to please ride with us. I had to go it alone. You said You have a horse because You have told me You are coming back on one, a pure white one at that. So I imagine you are riding in front of us and looking back periodically to smile and laugh encouragement to us.

I had just started my ride out by the big irrigation holding pond when Paladin suddenly locked up all fours. There was a black dog standing stock still in the shadow of a tree. He had been in the water and was glistening wet. To top it off, he had a gigantic stick in his mouth. This translated to the horse's mind as--DEMON! If the dog had just moved a little, the horse would have figured out what it was. But black dog's owners thought they were doing us a favor by playing statue. Wrong! Equine panic mode ensued. He even tried to buck and then tried to bolt. I kept saying, "Whoa! You're all right!" And of course I said it loudly and over and over. I always yell when I am afraid and was sure I was going to come off. I applied the training tool of the one rein stop, holding that right rein up short and turning, spinning on him at least five full circles. I really thought it was over and all my work up to this point was going to be lost. I was so scared.

But he finally stopped and settled.

The dog and his people moved on, rattled as well, shaking their heads over such a crazy horse and its screaming rider. I wanted to get off, lead him back home and never get on again. Instead I continued my ride and put him into a trot away from home's direction for the longest stretch we've ever done, figuring he needed to release some of that pent up tension. I know I did. The aftermath of my adrenalin helped me push him hard and forward. Strangely, that lent me some confidence. We had a successful ride after that, even getting lost a little on a different trail and having fun (did I just say, "fun?") finding our way back. I think this was quite a breakthrough, but I sure didn't enjoy the incident as it was happening.

Dear Successful One,

I was there with you and My hand was on him, too. I needed you to have a bit of a test there to apply what you have been learning. Don't you appreciate that one rein stop tool? Gets his focus on you up there in the saddle and off the object of his terror. Keeps his feet moving and not bucking. He needs to understand things are often not what they appear.

And so do you.

Take that into account when you perceive what might be happening in the shadowy corners of your life walk. Calm down. It likely is not the threat your enemy, Satan, is portraying it to be. Even if it were, I AM is here *and greater is I AM who is in you than he who is in the world.* When you asked me into your heart as Lord and Savior, I came and with Me I brought all that I AM. *In this world, while you remain in it, you will have difficulties that are very real indeed, but you can be of good cheer in the middle of them because I overcame the entirety of this world system. I said on the cross, "It is finished!" And so, it is. I am over all and in all. Everything is Mine to command.*

When the scary thing approaches or is detected in the shadows, don't run away. Don't get in fear. Listen for instructions. Turn and focus your mind's eye on Me. *I will help you, I will instruct you. I will uphold you with my righteous right hand.* Listen, I say, to my Voice. I might tell you to sidestep away or back up slowly while still facing the disconcerting trouble. Or I might tell you to turn and go another pathway. Or maybe I will ask you to face it down and herd it away. Yes, sometimes I may even ask you to run from a situation, but never in panic.

Never turn and bolt in fear and resistance to My Voice. Never get mad and "buck," so to speak, as if I am crazy *holding your feet to the path.* If you do, whether the object of your fear is real or not, it will have you in its destructive power and you will become a danger to yourself and to others as well.

Learn to pause first and listen. Yes, *I can even stop the clock* (have you noticed how time seems to stop when an accident is about to happen?) and give you space to see it and know exactly what it is and what to do about it. I will protect you. The scary thing is not scary to Me. Trust Me with the stuff in the shadows. Obey directional cues and you will not only survive, you will conquer.

Love,

Your Masterful Lord Who Rides A White Horse

I John 4:4; John 16:33; 19:30; Ephesians 4:6;
Isaiah 41:10; Proverbs 4:25-26; Joshua 10:12-14
Revelation 19:11-16

The dog stood stock still in the shadows

CHAPTER EIGHTEEN

LOOSEN UP

And David danced
before the Lord with all his might.
II Samuel 6:14a

Dear Lord,

All my trainers said that when the horse gets locked up in fear, get him to move his feet somewhere, anywhere; just move him so all four feet stay on the ground. I certainly had a first hand experience when we encountered that dog! If the feet are locked up then so is his mind. When you don't have his feet or his mind, you have no control of what happens next and a wreck will likely ensue. It makes sense. I am trying to learn how to stop and let him look at things he is concerned about out on the trail while at the same time knowing when it is time to move his feet forward so he doesn't get in frozen fear mode.

Dear Jewel of My Heart,

Yes, this is so true. You, also, many times react to bad news by locking up inside with fear. You perceive what is happening must be beyond My help. You instantly think of Me far away, billions of miles into the heavens. You forget about Me being with you and in you. You become tense, angry, and full of strife looking only at the problem and not at Me, the solution. It paralyzes your soul.

When uncertain or in doubt about what is happening in your life, start a little dance in your spirit. King David did when he "*encouraged himself in the Lord.*" Then let that little dance move into your feet. Start to praise Me with your mouth and move your mind toward My heart. Then your soul will begin to free up more and focus on Me, your strong leader *for Whom nothing is too hard.*

Tension locks you up. Worry takes you captive. Fear pulls you into a black hole.

Think! Remember! I have brought you through so much already in your life! Allow gratitude to swell up and break these chains. *I AM able to keep you from falling.* Oh that my followers would dance more before Me and with Me and be less regimented by what is happening in the world! The enemy of your soul can't stomach a dancing believer in Me, especially when all the circumstances look very grim. Remember, appearances often are deceptions when Satan is at work *stealing, killing and destroying.*

With any sort of trial, be sure to look to Me first. Trust in Me. Just like you want your horse to do with you. I will steer you in the right direction at the right time in the midst of the situation if you pay attention. Trust!

I live in your heart of hearts. *Out of it flow the wellsprings of life.*

Praise! I await you on the dance floor, my love.

Jehovah Nissi,

The Lord, your Banner

I Samuel 30:6; 2 Corinthians 1:2-7; Jeremiah 32:17;
Jude 1:24-25; John 10:10; Proverbs 4:23;
Exodus 17:15

CHAPTER NINETEEN

THE JOY OF JOINING IN

…"Truly, truly I say to you,
the Son can do nothing of his own accord;
but only what he sees the Father doing,
For whatever the Father does, that the Son does likewise."
John 5:19

Dear Friend Jesus,

Today when I went out to the corral to do some groundwork with Paladin, I asked You as usual what You wanted to teach us this time. We have those blue water barrels and the orange traffic cones and logs and things to work with. I wanted to move the barrels so I turned one on its side and began to roll it away. Paladin was on the lead line walking behind me but then he came up beside me and started to "help" using his knees and nose to push it. So amazing and unexpected! It took me by surprise. The things he used to avoid and even fear he seems have decided have no power over him and he can safely touch and herd them away. What new confidence is this! How I laughed and enjoyed that moment! He looked so pleased with himself.

Dear Delightful Daughter,

What a breakthrough! What a huge step in his trust of you! In other words, if he sees you doing something then it must be safe for him to join in and do it, too.

You are moving into the next level with Me as well. This is where we become partners in prayer, shifting things in the spiritual realm and consequently on the earth for My Kingdom purposes. You watch me work and you join in to help. I rejoice when you have grown in your confidence in Me, coming alongside Me in My work. I remind you again, don't yield to fear. Move the scary objects. Don't let them move you. You will see them finally for what they really are. Keep them exposed and move them out of the way. Move doubt, move sickness, move debt, move trouble, yes--even move demons that harass my people. *I have given you all power over the enemy in My Name.* But don't act on your own. Come alongside Me because you trust Me and you really want to be with Me. You trust that I know what I AM doing. I delight for you to help Me in My work, reaching out to the lost and forgotten, the hopeless and helpless.

In Me you live and move and have your being. Watch Me and then do what I am doing.

I enjoy you so much! *Let's move some mountains together!*

Love,

The Always Working One

James 4:7; Luke 10:17, 19-20;
Acts 17:28a; Matthew 17:20; 21:21

CHAPTER TWENTY

FOLLOW THE LEADER

My sheep hear my voice
and I know them,
and they follow Me.
John 10:27

In March of 2010 we began yet another spirited spring riding season. As usual, after a winter off, we both did the "fear freeze," but more easily pushed it aside this time. We started again with groundwork warm-ups and once more sought new people to ride with. It was incredible to me that the ones I counted on for riding buddies were not available consistently. I concluded that women who rode horses were either not reliable, or they grew tired of the upkeep and sold their horses after a couple of years, or maybe they simply became bored with my chatty conversations and slower pace. Finding no one right away, I asked the Lord what I should do and He reminded me how I trained my other horse, Legacy, when he was a youngster and yet not ride able. I then pondered how he and I had done a lot of walking the trails together with only a halter and lead rope. Legacy became very accustomed to everything that could and would pop up along the way, and by the time he was three, had learned to look to me as his leader. Our trails at that time were in suburban Seattle, Washington. We would walk side by side together for three or four miles, stopping in various places along the way looking at potentially scary things and facing sudden encounters of bicycles, strollers, dogs, large trucks, thunderstorms and wind blown monsters on trash days. We shared granola bars, good conversations and camaraderie. Trust in one another was the result. When it came time to put on a saddle and ride him, he was more than ready to be my safe mount. He knew I would take good care of him and I never had behavior issues with him.

Paladin and I had skipped this very important step. It was a "hole," so to speak, in his training. Most likely no one had ever taken the time to slow down with him and get this foundation. Grateful for this wisdom from God, I realized this gap must be filled in, and it was something we could do without another rider with us.

Dear Wise Lord,

Here I am again; ready to start riding the big Paladin, the mighty Mr. P. There he is again, with head up to the sky having to learn the same lessons from the last three years. Yet I see he settles much more quickly into each thing I ask of him in the groundwork. It would seem he is actually enjoying his drama of pretending to be afraid. I see through it now. But it is still not what I need, that's for sure. Every riding season I can't help but wish I just had a quiet, boring horse to pull out of the mothballs and mosey along--just mosey. Am I done yet? Have I learned enough about myself? Is it time for him to move on to another owner? I am so tired of being afraid to ride because he acts so ferocious every spring. Steve observes and says it is like saddling up a T-Rex. You are probably tired of me saying this every year, too. Winters are simply too harsh to keep riding year round. Will he and I ever become one in mind and purpose? Will the drama never end?

Dear Riding Buddy,

The big P is calling your bluff. Again.

That's what fear does. And although it is taking up less and less percentage of storage space in your mind, as long as it is there, My perfect love is not complete in you. Perfect, you say? I didn't say *you* were perfect in allowing my love to reign in your heart and mind. I said My *love* is perfect in getting you to do so. Because *it drives out all fear.* Why can you not see and be thankful for all the progress that has been made? Think on this!

The dramatic, large brown horse is not afraid of you anymore. Remember how afraid he used to be? He even trusts you more than you know. But he is testing you as a worthy leader. Are you going to lead? If you don't, he will. And he is, well, a horse. You have to ride with authority now. Don't be afraid of him. I see more than a glimmer of love in him for you. How about that? Yes, believe it! Don't you think the love I am changing you with is having an effect on this my created horse as well? Remember, in your mind and as you train him, carry a *rod and a staff* like I do, the former for protection and driving off predators and the other for merciful correction. Both ensure respect. He must respect you as leader. Take him out to the trails. Don't ride for the next several times. Just walk ahead and lead him. Put on all his tack and take him on some adventures. Then ride a little. Alternate walking and riding. Let him know you go before him, blazing the trail with great confidence! Lead from the ground. Then you can lead from the saddle. This leadership part of his training has been missing. It is a "hole" in his mind. Let's fill that hole with some more trust in you.

I do that for you. I AM your *pillar of fire by night and your pillar of cloud by day.* I AM ever leading. I AM confident. I AM bold. I AM authoritative. I chase devils out of the way, sure of the path, *knowing where to stop and rest,* happy to be with you and so pleased you are following along. I speak words of encouragement. I AM unafraid! *I AM the Bread of Life,* sharing my own self with you as we go.

And so you learn the sound of My Voice and the cadence of my footsteps. Know *I AM with you everywhere you go* whether you see Me or not.

Be the leader. But be a good leader. Be like Me.

Remember, I love you and I ride with you. Put on all *your* "tack" on your spiritual walk: *My Salvation for your helmet, My righteousness for your breastplate, Faith as your shield, your feet shod with the shoes of the*

Good News about My peace and be sure to put on the belt of Truth so you can be ready with the sword of My Spirit which is My written Word. I have many who are wandering around lost in their self-seeking ways. I want you to help them, lead them, and show them the path of light and life.

Come, let's take a walk together. We'll just mosey. There is no hurry.

And don't forget to pack the granola bar.

Love,

Your Leader, Worthy of all Trust

I John 4:18; Psalm 23:4; Exodus 13:21;
John 6:35; Deuteronomy 31:6; Hebrews 13:5;
Ephesians 6:14-17

CHAPTER TWENTY-ONE

LOOKING OR WATCHING?

Unless the Lord watches over the city,
the watchman stays awake in vain.
Psalm 127:1b

The leadership lessons impacted our rides significantly toward the positive. Paladin seemed to enjoy our walks out on the trails and learned to relax at the furthest points of the journey where I would break out the granola bar and share it with him. I relaxed a lot also and soon I was alternating walking ahead of him with riding him, varying the times of each and the distance covered, and the locations. I began to have confidence riding without another rider along. In fact, I began to prefer it. However, we still had those "moments" when he was deciding whether to trust my judgment or not.

Dear Jesus,

Lord, sometimes when we are out riding the trails Paladin will suddenly tense, stop and raise up his head to stare off in a particular direction. I urge him on, but he ignores me and I tense up, too. Should I get off then? I see or hear nothing approaching. Realizing he has a far better sense of danger than I do makes me suspicious. I remember Linda saying that he is the kind of horse who is a real "lookee-loo." A worrier. Yeah, like me, right? The way out of it, she said, is to always look where he is looking. That way he knows that I know there might be something out there and maybe we should go away from it. Real or imagined, it is important to him that I do not ignore his suspicions. As I look, breathe and relax my seat, he too relaxes. Though it seems an eternity, it is really only a few seconds. It is like I must communicate the message: "Even though I am quite sure there is nothing harmful out there, I respect your notion that there is. I am ready to avoid it or kill it, whatever it is. I've got your back. My perspective is clear from up here. You can trust me."

Dearest Lookee-loo,

Yes, I AM teaching you the difference between "looking" and "watching." The former is done without involving wisdom and generally involves fear of what could be. The latter involves seeing with discernment. Foolish reactions stem from simply looking. Watching employs wisdom, which leads to understanding of the situation.

He wants to know you are keeping watch over him while you ride. Listen, turn and look in all directions now and then when all is relaxed and going forward. Pat him on the hindquarters as you turn and look back. Stroke his neck as you look side to side. He will begin to learn you are not simply looking around randomly but really watching steadily and calmly. When something does pop up from the bushes--a dog, rabbit, deer or another rider-- he will take it in stride because he has been listening to you. Fear must take a back seat in both of your minds. Remember, My perspective above you is accurate and *My Goodness and Mercy are continually following you.*

I am not one to say when the wolf comes, "Look out, sheep! Run for your lives!" and then dash away from them leaving them scattered to the wolves' destruction. No, *I am the Good Shepherd* who stands to defend the sheep against the enemy. I have their backs.

You literally have the back of your timid horse. He grows ever more confident in your confidence. As for you, are you looking for hardships, dark things and dangers in this life all the time? Do you anticipate just because you heard some rumor? Or are you watching *with* Me, noticing my Spirit's settled demeanor? I am the Watchman on the wall of your life. Trust My love to guide My clear perspective of things seen and unseen.

Looking is often initiated by fear.

Watching is always initiated and guided by wisdom.

Watch with Me. Sing with Me while we ride together:

> *"When peace, like a river, attendeth my way,*
> *When sorrows like sea billows roll;*
> *Whatever my lot, Thou has taught me to say,*
> *It is well, it is well, with my soul"*

Love,
Your Good Shepherd

Psalm 23:6; John 10:11

CHAPTER TWENTY-TWO

ADVANCEMENT

When they went,
they went in any of their four directions
without turning as they went.
Ezekiel 1:17

During the summer and fall of this same year I continued a few lessons out at Bill's ranch. He had developed some of his land into a trail course with various obstacles and other "tests" of trail riding, much like the indoor course Paladin had completed with such flying colors back in 2006. Bill could teach his students and the young horses he also trained to gain skill and confidence for real-time trail rides. Honing my developing trail riding abilities under a trainer's skilled eye was always a good thing for Paladin and me to do, and we still did not do any cantering on our trail rides so I thought this should be the year to start learning. It was a real roadblock for me as I couldn't stop fearing he would go into a buck if I asked him to canter. There were also trail skills like side-passing we needed to master.

Dear Jesus, Instructor,

Today Bill asked me to learn to side-pass on him. Wow, it is enough just to get on and ride in a straight line. Now I have to cue him with leg and reins to move his whole body to the left or right, but when I do he either tries to go forward or backward instead. I have to stop his forward movement with the reins and his backward movement with my legs and all very quickly but subtlety, of course. This is very frustrating for him as well because he starts swishing and wringing his tail in irritation at my amateur signals. I am sure he will buck me off again. He knows how to do all this stuff but I don't! He has no patience with me and I don't blame him. I cannot get the hang of asking him correctly. This side-pass thing is an important maneuver out on the trails. Sometimes a rider and horse can find themselves stuck going over a log or brush and the only way out is to step sideways—calmly. Calmly? That will be the day…!

Dear Not A Quitter,

This definitely takes more skill. You have to learn how to ask right and he needs to know what you are asking for. It will come. Just practice. Don't push him on it too long and get him upset. You are the one getting upset by the way. If I had given you a tail, you would be wringing it. Remember, he reads you in an instant and because of his quickness, he knows what you are thinking even before you do.

I, too, want to take you and all my people into advanced training. In the deeper walk with Me you will learn how to be more than two-dimensional. There is more to being a Christ follower than simply going to church! The realms of the Spirit are multi-dimensional. We do not move simply forward or backward here in the unseen. Read about it in Ezekiel.

When you are learning advanced lessons with Me and don't understand what I am asking you to do, simply quiet yourself and listen. I am extremely patient. You should know that by now, sweet girl. Sometimes I will give you a word or an impression. Learn to ask Me to discern--is it I or another voice? Move with Me. Remember The Dance lesson? *Anger and frustration must be put away from you.* You will only "get" it when you calm down and think about listening.

Side-pass left may be your need to go to someone and ask his or her forgiveness.

Side-pass right might be a sin to renounce in yourself.

Back up: There is generational bondage to be cut off.

Go forward quickly: Flee the enemy and his temptations.

Stand still: Settle down and be quiet before Me. Hold your ground.

Remember, to side-pass is to advance just as much as going forward. Let Me flow through you with My commands. *I will teach you My ways, show you My paths and lead you in My Truth.*

Love,

Your Yeshua, Advancing The Kingdom of God

Ezekiel 1:15-21, I Peter 5:7; James 1:19, Psalm 25:4

Paladin and I had to learn how to sidepass over a log

CHAPTER TWENTY-THREE

BACKSLIDING

For the righteous falls seven times and rises again,
but the wicked stumble in times of calamity.
Proverbs 24:16

Later this same year, one of my solo rides on Paladin proved greatly disturbing. I did not feel safe...again! He was so full of himself that day. When I pulled back on the reins, he wouldn't stop. When I turned him in circles to slow him down, he spun faster. When I got off and made him lunge in circles, he wouldn't look at me, but just ran around crazily. It was a really rotten ride. There was no reason I could think of why he would suddenly pull the same disobedient antics on me that he had tried early on in his training. Everything I had worked for, everything we had accomplished so far seemed to vanish. Was I back at square one with him? I was so very discouraged. He had failed me. He had rebelled and I vowed it would be the last time. I was done with this horse for sure. Life was too short.

Dear Papa,

That's it!
This horse and I are through! It is time for us to part ways. You saw how he acted and then ignored me? It was like we just threw the last three years on the manure pile and ran over them with the tractor!

After all I have done for him! After all the time, energy, tears and throwing aside my fears every time to get on and ride! Maybe there is something here You want to teach me, but I have to say, I just do not get it! My heart is like a cold stone toward him. I feel betrayed.

Dear Persistent One,

You are still afraid. He is tired of it. So am I. You know very well how horses pick up on your emotional state. You are responding in anger--again. So is he. Well, what should I do with the both of you? Shall I write you off and walk away? Do I throw up my hands in disgust and go find someone else more worthy of My time? Do I deny my very nature? My love is multifaceted, like a diamond in the sunlight. One of the dimensions is long-suffering. Of course there is a lesson I am bringing to you in this: I am teaching you to be like Me. I am developing and reshaping your reactive human nature.

There are times when I tell you to "do this" and not to "do that." For a while you comply in obedience. But then you rebel by ignoring my commands. You backslide into old patterns. One would think, with all the time I invest in training my people that they would never fall back into doing things their own way instead of My way. One would think, with all the blessings strewn on the path of obedience that my people would never want to charge off on their own trail. One would think...but they don't think. And surely they don't think right.

Do I give up on you? Do I say, "That's it! Enough of teaching her! We're selling you down the road, sister!"

No. My hand is always open to you, right in the midst of your self-serving actions. Focus on yourself and you will stay in fear and anger. Focus on Me and we will keep stripping away these hazards.

I went to the cross for friends who deserted Me after I spent three years teaching, loving, training and cultivating relationship with them. I invested all of Myself in them and they ran the other way. I could easily have deserted them that day and been well within my "rights."

I AM the Son of God, after all. Papa God and I are One. *Legions of angels were waiting to get Me out of there.*

Perfect Love bid Me die for them so that they and all others after them who believe in Me could have eternal life. I AM the connection to a Holy God. Obedience was a choice. Do you think that was easy?

I never give up on you. Get back to your trainer, Bill, who I am using to help you. How could you possibly give up on your brown horse now after all you have learned together? *Do you not know that suffering produces endurance and endurance produces character and character produces hope and hope does not disappoint?* Keep going with your handsome, and yes, rebellious horse. Have you noticed his coat in the sunlight, how it is now tinged with gold from all the good nutrition you have been feeding him? Gold is not shiny and beautiful until it is starting to exhibit the refinement process. He is not reverting back to who he was but he has a layer of dross that is about to fall off. It is the same with you.

Remember, I AM teaching you. *You are my friend if you do what I tell you.*

Love,

The One Who Never Gives Up

Matthew 26:53; John 3:16; Romans 5:4; John 5:14

CHAPTER TWENTY-FOUR

BREAKDOWN TO BREAKTHROUGH

"And why does God let troubles come?
God harnesses trouble, puts a bit in its mouth, and makes it obey Him,
and those troubles bring us into a closer fellowship with God."[vi]
-William Branham

Back to Bill we went who, with a casual shrug, just stated the horse was feeling a little frisky. The weather was cool and frosty. Add in some fresh, sugary shoots of new spring grass and a horse's energy level will run a little high. It was no big deal, he assured me. However, at the start of our third lesson we rode out on his trail course and he asked me to put the horse into a canter. OK, I thought, I can do this. Forgetting about everything (like staying loose and relaxed) but the task at hand, I sucked in my breath and gave Paladin a half-hearted kick with my feet. This resulted in the horse doing a little crow hop (i.e., a half hearted buck). Flashing back to the first damaging ride on him, I didn't even try to stay on and slid to the ground, butt first. By doing so, I risked my foot becoming stuck in the stirrup and getting dragged, head banging along on the ground. But to come off slowly seemed better than to get bucked off.

I managed to keep my foot with me and Paladin ran off merrily, heading for a busy highway, tail and head held high. To me, it was an instant replay of what had taken place that day in 2006. Bill put his horse into a slow lope and headed after him. Fortunately, Paladin stopped at Bill's corral to visit with some other horses and I didn't have to contend with a traffic accident, too.

When Bill brought him back to the place where I had been dislodged, he found me steaming with anger and frustration. Why after all this time had he tried to buck? I was done with him. Oh yes, this time no one, not even God Himself was going to talk me into ever riding this horse again! "It was just a little buck, scarcely could be called a buck," Bill said, addressing the fear in my face, "Even if you *are* done with him, you have to get on again," he insisted." I said "no" three times and he said "yes" four times so I got back on. "Foolish idiot," I said to myself, "just leave him here and let Bill find him another home with someone else."

We rode out at a walk and trot, and after riding for about 30 minutes came back toward the same spot where I had fallen. As we approached I set my jaw in determination, took a big breath in *and* out and pushed him forward into a canter for a few paces. He didn't buck. We had a nice, short gallop together. I stayed on and Bill praised us both heartily.

Ah, I sighed happily. Breakthrough!

Dear Lord,

Did you see that? I was so disgusted with the whole situation of him acting up and me being afraid that I shoved the fears aside and made him do the right thing. Or did I make *myself* do the right thing?

Dear Cowgirl,

Yes! Way to take authority over fear! You do not need to flee your fears. *They will flee from you* when you sit up and ride! You needn't have fallen off the first time in this lesson today except that you got into fear thoughts again. And you held your breath.

Listen to My word given to another one of my daughters and learn:

"I know it is hard to fall off your horse and get back on. And we do give you time to recover - and, yes, even when you feel the need to keep your head buried for a while. But, precious, you must breathe and come up for air.

Stand up dear one, and return to obedience to what I have told you. Stand up beloved, and climb back on. Honor My prophetic Word over your life, for it will go well with thee.

It is only in serving Me that you will find the grace to overcome all that assails you. Stretch forth the rod I have given you and walk in the authority to which I have called you. As you walk the path of your destiny, I AM carrying you upon My own back. It is a balancing act not to fall off, but I AM not running, I AM walking. One day at a time, Precious, simply walk with Me. The angels rejoice as you are willing to get up and move forward. 'Up and at 'em, let's go.'"[vii]

Why are you still so afraid of danger when I AM is with you? Launch out into the deep, ride out into the storm. Centered on Me you cannot fail. You will not be unseated when *you are seated with Me* and so you are! We will be able to accomplish a lot more for My Kingdom when you can move a little faster. Keep practicing! *Banish the fear and doubt.*

Love,

President, Riders on the Storm Club

James 4:7; Matthew 21:21; Ephesians 2:6

101

Paladin ran off merrily, heading for a busy
highway, tail and head held high.

CHAPTER TWENTY-FIVE

ARE YOU BREATHING?

Whoever believes in Me, as the scripture has said,
'Out of his heart will flow rivers of living water'
John 7:38

I rode the rest of 2010 into the fall without any more issues with Paladin. He was good and steady as we rode mostly without other riders on the trails. I still did not have the courage to gallop unaccompanied by Bill so we just enjoyed walking and a good long trot at times.

As January of 2011 approached, I began to plan another riding season. The Lord brought to mind a book in my library called *Centered Riding* by Sally Swift. [viii] It had been a long time since I had read it. Knowing I would face another "fresh" Paladin come spring, I dusted it off and set out to find an instructor in this particular discipline. Asking around our "horsey" network I found a woman trained and certified. Incredibly, she lived only a few miles away. Weekly lessons were set up in an available indoor arena which was also close to home like the one I had used earlier in his training, I would be able to trailer slowly over ice and snow if such arose.

Our new trainer again began both of us on the ground, out of the saddle to see what our individual tension levels were and to explain many things about being "centered" in the core of our bodies. If I braced in tension, it would cause me to rise up into my shoulders and upper body which was unbalanced and top heavy. When the horse braced, the same thing happened to his body and his energy would be all up in his back and neck instead of down in his feet. This set up a dangerous combination which could easily lead to such discomfort for the horse that he would want me off, using whatever means necessary (think: bucking). We then worked on correct breathing and balance under saddle. I wondered why I had not done this kind of training before all the others.

The principles of this method of horseback riding helped me to understand much about my relationship with Paladin and quickened my heart to new revelation about my relationship with the Lord. Was I living by fear or by trust? Were my mind and heart centered in the "core" of my spirit where Jesus lived by means of His Holy Spirit? Was I balanced on both feet in life, grounded in God's Truths and applying them to my life?

Dear Lord,

Thank you for leading me back to this amazing book. Riding is much more than sitting on a horse and being carried around. It is about being aware, being aligned and simply breathing (of all things!) It is about truly being one with the horse and him with me. If I hold my breath, so does he. If I tense my shoulders, so does he. If I ride down deep into my seat and feet by breathing into them, the cadence of his feet becomes relaxed and he listens to me better. I am amazed by how much I hold my breath even when I am *not* riding. Wow. What an eye opener this is. As I feel more secure and balanced, he relaxes his neck, back and head. Our center of gravity simultaneously becomes lower into our feet. As we did this at one point we both let out this long exhale at exactly the same time! As I relaxed my rib cage by breathing from my diaphragm instead of my chest, my legs became softer around *his* rib cage and he had more room to breathe. I felt my breath go right down and through his body. How uncomfortable it must have been for him to feel my legs clamped tight on his sides! Years of trying to hang on that way and trying to control a horse with my hands and head were actually making me unsafe. Revelation: I am such a control freak!

Dear Centered Daughter,

Uncomfortable, isn't it, when you are all up in your shoulders thinking you are in control? I put the brain in the head not because it is to be the place of balance but because it crowns the real center of life, the soul that is at rest in Me. Man's reasoning is futile apart from Me. In your heart of hearts, where your life is hidden with me is where *you live and move and have your being.* My Holy Spirit indwells you, guides you and helps you. As you check in with Me often, especially during fearsome situations in this world, I re-center you with My Truth and balance. There is where you are grounded and unshakeable. This takes much practice. You forget and get "all up in arms" so to speak when circumstances seem to prevail. You lose confidence in Me because your attention is on the thing happening to you. You become un-centered and unbalanced. Take heart! Through our work with this wonderful horse you are learning more and more to come to Me quickly when perplexed or fearful. You see now how he responds quickly to you when you simply breathe correctly and let go of your desire to control things.

Take a deep breath beloved, more often. I AM the Breath of Life. Breathing from the center of your inner being where I live will cause you to hear Me and *be content in all situations.* Fear causes you to have tension in your focus like the author of the book teaches, resulting in tunnel vision, which creates nothing more than an empty hollow resounding with a lying echo that I won't take care of you. Centering your trust continually on Me will cause your spiritual vision to be fully peripheral. Though you see the trial at hand you will also become aware of the bigger picture. Remember what I have told you earlier: things are not always what they appear. Say to your self again, "fear is false evidence appearing real!" Never, ever forget this. Don't rise up in tension. Come down; come down my strong one into your center where I AM. There is where I guide you continually.

Guide your good horse this way. He has no tolerance for tension in you. That is why I brought him to you, to teach you about your problem with that and how it totally interferes with being one with

Me. As you learn to flow with him and he with you, you will begin to understand the mighty flow of My Spirit in you. Others need to *taste and see that* I *AM good.* How will they learn that from you if you are blocked up with fear and tension?

BREATHE, BALANCE, ALIGN, PERCEIVE. Let go, dear heart, and ride secure.

Love,

Your Lord,

Command Central

Acts 17:28; Philippians 4:11; Psalm 34:8

CHAPTER TWENTY-SIX

<u>SETTLED</u>

I will say to the Lord,
"My refuge and my fortress,
My God,
In Whom I trust."
Psalm 91:2

Dear Lord,

Thank you for helping me to see my faults and shortcomings in such a loving way. How can I bring *You* joy this day? I get so ready to give up on this horse when he doesn't seem to appreciate anything I do for him. I know I am that way with You--resistant, rebellious, ungrateful and untrustworthy, yet You never turn away from me. Forgive me for first responding in fear and anger instead of in trust in You. Forgive me for being self-centered instead of Christ-centered.

Willing consistency is what I ask You to give Paladin so he becomes a joy to ride. Consistent trust is what I ask You to continue to develop in me so I become a joy for You to be with.

I wanted so much to replace this horse with another more reliable one. Please forgive *my* unreliability. You could easily have found someone else to do what I am supposed to do for Your Kingdom but you patiently persisted with me, and continue to do so. Forgive me for bracing against Your commands and Your love, for they are one and the same. Help me to completely yield to You.

I ask that in Paladin's horsey brain You would manifest the attitude that all is well. His owner, his keeper is here with him and I will not ask of him anything beyond what he is created for. Help me to bring him to a place in his mind where my voice alone will settle him in any situation. Likewise in my human mind, I ask that You would do the same. All is well. *I will say of the Lord He alone is my refuge*, my leader, my keeper, my hope, my comforter, my protector and my teacher. I will not be afraid nor will I rebel. I will yield myself more and more to You, Lord, in every situation, throughout every day. I will trust so I might bring You joy, *making Your joy complete*.

Dear Beloved One,

I AM THE LORD, slow to anger and abounding in steadfast mercy. I never give up. I call the prodigal until he comes home. I pursue the one lost sheep until I find it. I carry the weak one in My arms. I AM patience. I AM kindness. I AM goodness. I AM faithfulness. I AM peace. I AM Joy. I AM love. I bear all things. I believe all things. I hope all things. I endure all things. My love never fails.

Just receive.

Respond in love. Don't react in fear. All is well. You are perfectly loved.

Love,

Your Savior

Exodus 34:6; Psalm 91:2; John 3:29; I Corinthians 13
Luke 15; I Corinthians 13:7,8; Isaiah 40:11;
Galatians 5:22; John 16:24

CHAPTER TWENTY-SEVEN

CARRY MY NAME

And on that day there shall be inscribed on
the bells of the horses,
"Holy to the Lord."
Zechariah 14:20a

Dear Warrior Daughter,

I said to you as we began this journey, "You are just like this horse." And so you are. See how he has changed because you have changed. My *love for you is indeed perfect and it has and always will drive out all fear.* Fear, driven away, carries out on its back *anger, bitterness, wrath, and unkindness* to name just a few destructive emotions. To forgive must first of all be a choice far above any and all emotional support; it all starts with forgiving those who wrong you when you do not *feel* like forgiving.

As you stood in front of his stall that day over five years ago and lashed out your hatred for this horse I created, I wrapped you both together in my loving arms. I gave you the choice to let Me begin to retrain you or leave you as you were. He would have gone off to auction and be further treated with cruelty and you would still be thinking it is OK to live with that constant underlying fear that has been with you since childhood.

That was not OK with Me.

Fear breeds destruction. My Love casts it out. I redeem, renew and rebuild. See how willingly and happily blessed Paladin carries you up and down the trails now. Observe how he listens to you when the unexpected happens along the trail. Notice the way he settles as you relax your seat and legs when things get tense around you. Appreciate the soft blowing from his nostrils as he seeks peace in your breath blowing back at him. Rejoice in his glad nickering when he sees you coming each morning.

He trusts you now.

I also am observing how you are listening to Me so much more when the unexpected happens. I am noticing the way you are learning to settle down and check in with Me when things get tense around you. I appreciate the way you are seeking My peace first and foremost each day. I rejoice in your praise of Me as you see Me coming to you with your spiritual eyes and hear Me with spiritual ears. One day you will see Me face to face.

You are trusting Me. Now carry My Name proudly, happily, boldly in the *strength of My joy. To those who honor My Name, I, the Son of Righteousness, will rise with healing in My wings and you will go out and find good pasture.*

Thank you for staying the course with him. I love you both so much. We are not done. The trail goes on for a ways yet. There are many more twists and turns, lessons in denying fear and acting in love. Stay centered on Me. Carry My Name into this broken, frozen in fear world. Offer the hope of Salvation to those made in My image. Breathe in My peace. Breathe out My love.

Love,

Your Warrior King Jesus

I John 4:18; Ephesians 4:31,32;
Malachi 4:2; John 10:9

CHAPTER TWENTY-EIGHT

A MORE PERFECT LOVE

For now we see in a mirror dimly, but then face to face.
Now I know in part;
Then I shall know fully, even as I have been fully known.
I Corinthians 13:12

"I love you sweet boy," I said quietly.

Standing in front of Paladin's stall on a bright, late summer day in 2011, I realized the confidence we had developed in one another. I wasn't angry and he wasn't afraid. He had learned to trust a human again and I had learned to become trustworthy by trusting more in the One who loved us both.

I lifted my hand to his head, resting it between his ears. He didn't throw it up high like he used to. Instead, he slowly lowered it, and as he did, I pressed my forehead against his. "Good boy," I whispered over and over again. A huge sigh came through his whole body and blew softly out through his nostrils. His eyes closed contentedly and in that sigh I heard, "thank you."

"Good boy," I whispered. "Thank you for trusting me."

Dear Jesus,

Thank you. For You have changed me yet again to be more like You. None of this ever could have happened without the refining power of Your patient love. To think You would use a horse, an animal who is powerful enough to kill me but is willing to give up that power to have relationship with me, to teach me more about You and my partnership with You. I am so amazed and so grateful. I know this horse and I have much yet to learn. As I seek You each day in Your Word and in conversation with You constantly, I will continue on this path of learning to trust in You more. Thank You for always riding with me on this trail called life. Someday You will stop, turn around to smile at me and tell me we are Home and I will at last see You face to face, the One I have followed, the One I have learned to trust no matter what. I will then press my forehead against Yours where the scars still remain from the thorns You wore for me. And we will ride together on the wings of the morning.

Dearest Daughter Whom I love with all My Heart,

Thank you for learning to trust Me first instead of reacting in fear. It is always your freedom to choose. Indeed, on that Day, *To those who overcome, I will give them a white stone with a new name written on it that no one knows except those who receive it.* On that Day, you will know the name I have reserved just for you. While you journey with Me now, I call you an overcomer and my *friend.* I have taught you about love. It is the only remedy for fear. Though fears will still assail you on this side of life, cast them out one by one as you remind yourself of My love, love you don't always understand but love that trumps fear every time, for it is perfect and eternal.

Are we done yet? Not by any means. We will continue on. New trials await as long as you are in this fallen world. Stay with Me. Stay under Me. *Abide, dwell, remain in Me.* Remember, *he who dwells in the secret place of the Most High will abide in the shadow of the Almighty.*

Have you noticed your excelling new compassion, love and patience for all My people? I have been forming My own likeness in your heart of hearts. Those made in My image are exceedingly more obstinate and harder to train than many horses put together! You have certainly found this to be true of yourself and your horse! Go now, take the refining I have done in your heart and share it with my lost and hurting ones. Tell them they too can learn to forgive themselves and others who have greatly wronged them. Tell them I am not mad at them. Speak my love to them. Help them invite Me into the round pens of their lives, allowing Me to have My gentle, firm and effective way with them. Show them how to let Me take the reins of their lives. Explain to them how to become one with Me. Assure them I AM trustworthy. I whisper their names.

I am Jesus, their Savior. I love them with an everlasting Love. Teach them to start their training with Me by saying, "Jesus, come into my life. Be my Lord and Savior. I can't do this by myself. I am tired of running in circles that go nowhere. I want to follow You. Take off this heavy load of fear I carry. I trust You now by faith that You will come into my heart and lead me and refine me to trust all You have planned for me to be."

You see, *all creation is currently looking for the sons of God to be revealed.* They are looking for Me in people like you who follow Me as Savior and Lord and allow My love to shine out from you. Fear blocks the shine. Refuse it when it comes.

My daughter, please enjoy to the fullest your big, shiny brown and white horse. *And I will ride with you always, even to the end of time.*

I LOVE YOU! And I trust you, too. Let's saddle up and go for a ride today!

Always and forever,

Yahweh—I AM THAT I AM

Your God and Father, Son and Holy Spirit

Revelation 2:17; John 15:4; Psalm 91:1;
Romans 8:22; Matthew 28:20; Exodus 3:14

They shall see his face,
and his name will be on their foreheads.
and night will be no more.
They will need no light of lamp or sun,
for the Lord God will be their light,
and they will reign forever and ever.
Revelation 22:4

ABOUT THE AUTHOR

Marie Timm grew up the youngest of four "preacher's kids" and was horse "crazy" from the start. Although her parents sympathized, they were not able to provide her a horse of her own. She devoured as many horse books as the local library had on the shelves and thought about little else in her younger years.

Encouraged to write creatively by her high school teachers, she set off for college, pen in hand. There she produced various poems and short stories in her English classes. It was the early 1970's and the environmental movement drew her in her sophomore year away from writing and into horticulture and the therapy plant care could provide to physically and mentally challenged persons.

Graduating with a Bachelor of Science degree in Horticultural Therapy, she was selected as one of only a handful of graduate students to intern at the famous Longview Gardens in Pennsylvania. Marie's love for her new fiancé, Steve proved to be a stronger pull and she put aside all to follow him to the Pacific Northwest where they began their life together. Two children came quickly along with several dogs, three horses and small stints of employment in the horticultural industry. The next 25 years was spent nurturing her family and moving frequently with Steve's career. Writing was always on the back burner but not addressed in any concrete way. Church, Bible studies and spiritual growth continued at a slow and steady pace. Her riding skills improved at various horse boarding and training facilities.

In 2001, a profound experience with God's Holy Spirit occurred at a four-day church retreat. Several weeks later she awoke one morning with the word, "Write" emblazoned on her mind and began to journal over the next several years. Still putting aside any public writing aspirations, she found herself standing in front of her new horse in 2006 hearing that Voice again. The One who had said, "Write!" years earlier. The One who had called her to help others under His inspiration. The One who calls each of us by name.

END NOTES

[i] Audrey Eddings, Wind of the Spirit Ministries, Silverdale, Washington

[ii] Dictionary.com, "if wishes were horses," in *The American Heritage®Dictionary of Idioms by Christine Ammer*. Source location: Houghton Mifflin Company. http://dictionary.reference.com/browse/if wishes were horses. Available: http://dictionary.reference.com. Accessed: October 14, 2013.

[iii] Helen H. Lemmel, 1922, *Turn Your Eyes Upon Jesus,* Public Domain

[iv] Marjorie Barrows, *Fraidy Cat*, (Rand McNally, 1943)

[v] Horatio G. Spafford, 1873, *It Is Well With My Soul*, Copyright: Public Domain

[vi] William Branham, Sermon Easter Sunday, *I Know*, Jefferson, Indiana

[vii] Sandy Warner, Word to Ponder: *When You Fall Off Your Horse*, 7/06/06, thequickenedword.com,

[viii] Sally Swift, *Centered Riding*, First Edition, A Trafalgar Square Farm Book, (David and Charles, Inc., North Pomfret, Vermont, St. Martin's/Marek,1985)